Treasures from the Burrell Collection

Hayward Gallery, London 18 March – 4 May 1975

Arts Council of Great Britain

Contents

Cover: Domenico Veneziano, *The Judgement of Paris* (cat. no.1)

© Arts Council 1975
Soft cover ISBN 0 7287 0046 8
Hard cover ISBN 0 7287 0045 X

A list of Arts Council publications, including
all exhibition catalogues in print, can be
obtained from the Publications Department,
Arts Council of Great Britain, 105 Piccadilly,
London W1V 0AU

Designed by Graham Johnson/Lund Humphries
Printed by Lund Humphries, London and Bradford

Acknowledgements

Great art collections and the personality of great collectors are endlessly fascinating even to those who have never felt the urge to collect, much less caught the fever in its more acute forms. Sir William Burrell was a chronic case who amassed a vast number of works of art of all kinds over a period of more than 50 years and who continued to 'round off' the collection in the years between giving it to the City of Glasgow in 1944 and his death in 1958. His intentions and the direction of his real interests as a collector remain obscure; his own records show that while his collecting was dominated by successive master interests, he consistently bought over a wide range of cultures at the same time. The principal rooms of his house, Hutton Castle, were hung with tapestries and filled with oak furniture on which stood 15th and 16th century carvings, and fine pieces of silver and pottery. Perhaps it is fair to assume that the middle ages were what he loved best and it is probably no coincidence that stained glass and tapestries are the most distinguished collections among his treasures.

In selecting this exhibition of a fraction of this treasure we considered that an attempt to be truly representative would be confusing and indigestible in the space at our disposal. Therefore we regretfully excluded silver, furniture, glass, needlework, armour, the Rodin bronzes, all pottery other than Chinese, to name some of the areas to which Sir William turned his attention.

We are greatly indebted to the Trustees of the Burrell Collection, to the Convenor and members of the Civic Amenities Committee of the City of Glasgow and to the Director of Glasgow Museums and Art Galleries, Mr. Trevor Walden, who responded so generously to our invitation to show part of the collection in London and who allowed us complete freedom of choice in the selection. In this we have been advised, from his unrivalled knowledge, by the Keeper of the Burrell Collection, Mr. William Wells, and by the following to whom we would like to express our thanks: for the tapestries and carpets Miss Wendy Hefford and Mr. David Sylvester, and for the Chinese bronzes and pottery Mr. Basil Gray.

The preparation of the exhibition and of this catalogue in a very short space of time have thrown a heavy burden on all those concerned with the collection and its conservation and we would like to thank particularly Mr. Wells for his extreme helpfulness and patience and for writing the catalogue at record speed; Mr. Alisdair Auld, Keeper of Fine Art, Glasgow Museums and Art Galleries; Miss Janet Notman, Senior Conservation Officer, and Mr. Harry McLean, Chief Conservation Officer, who have had to examine every object and picture to determine its fitness to travel; and Miss Flora Ritchie the Collection photographer.

Mr. Barry Gasson who, in association with Miss Brit Andresen is the architect for the new museum building, has designed the setting for this exhibition, assisted by Miss Alison McDonald. We are most grateful to them, and also to Miss Penelope Marcus who has edited the catalogue.

Robin Campbell
Director of Art

Joanna Drew
Director of Exhibitions

Foreword

by the Convener of the Civic Amenities Committee of the Corporation of Glasgow

The Corporation of Glasgow and the Burrell Trustees were both very pleased to accede to the Arts Council's request to stage this exhibition. For more than 30 years the greater part of this important collection has been stored away and some of it, particularly the splendid series of tapestries, has rarely been seen by the public. Although Sir William Burrell generously gave a sum of money which, at the time, would have gone some way towards providing a permanent home for the collection, difficulties in acquiring a site satisfying the stringent conditions of the trust deed delayed matters for many years. These difficulties were at last resolved when, in 1967, Mrs. Anne Maxwell Macdonald so generously gave the Pollok Estate to Glasgow. Within the 360 acres of parkland, only three miles from the city centre, was an ideal site meeting all the requirements and acceptable to the Burrell Trustees.

Plans for a new building to house the collection then went ahead quickly. A major architectural competition was sponsored and the winning design was widely acclaimed. The cost considerably exceeded the available Burrell funds but the Corporation was anxious to provide the new building and commissioned the architect to prepare working drawings ready for contract. These have just been completed and we are now eagerly waiting to hear from the Government what financial assistance will be forthcoming.

The Burrell Collection is of international importance but a whole generation has hardly seen it. It is part of the national heritage and Glasgow has a duty to make it available.

J. O'Sullivan
February 1975

Sir William Burrell

by William Wells

Sir William Burrell was one of the most remarkable collectors of the 19th and 20th centuries. He collected continuously and on a substantial, often breathtaking, scale of expenditure from about 1880 until his death in 1958, when he was 96. His collection amounting to about 8,000 items was of paintings, sculptures, tapestries, carpets, ceramics, metalwork and works of applied arts from a very wide range of cultures and historical periods. After presenting most of his collection to the City of Glasgow in 1944 Burrell set about forming a new one, and while maintaining his established interests was more concerned with the arts of ancient civilisations. These were added to the Collection he had given to Glasgow as he acquired them. He had already given £450,000 towards the cost of building a museum near Glasgow to house it.

Burrell was born in Glasgow on 9 July 1861, the third son of William Burrell and his wife, Isabella Duncan Guthrie. At the age of 15 he joined the family shipping firm, Burrell and Son. Together with his eldest brother he enlarged the business so successfully that at the height of its activity in 1915 the firm owned 30 ships all of over 4,000 gross tonnage. In 1917, however, Burrell decided to devote his interests to art and sold most of the fleet.

As a boy Burrell began collecting works of art and he claimed that his liking for art showed itself when he preferred to spend his pocket-money, to his father's annoyance, on a painting rather than on a cricket bat. Unfortunately, except for the works which he is known to have acquired, there is little information about how Burrell was assembling his collections before he was 50. But from 1911 he started to make entries of what he was acquiring in purchase books. These usually record a longer or shorter description and other details concerning provenance, payment, reception, insurance, and photography. Burrell became more and more aware of the value of documentation as the years went on and of the difficulty of distinguishing one object from others of a similar kind, if as the description in the purchase books omitted, as they tend to do in the earliest of them, the basic facts such as size. Burrell kept up the records himself until the last eighteen months of his life when they were completed by his housekeeper. His passion was such that he continued to add to his collection even when he was no longer able to record his purchases himself.

By 1901 Burrell was already an outstanding collector. In that year he lent over two hundred works to the big Glasgow International Exhibition: paintings, tapestries, carpets, needlework, furniture, woodcarvings, stained glass, glass vessels, metalwork, silver, ivories, alabasters, books, and a large miscellaneous

Numbers in square brackets refer to catalogue numbers

collection of art objects which were not itemised in the catalogue. Although in certain sections he was outclassed by other Scottish collectors, like Sir Thomas Gibson Carmichael whose collection of medieval metalwork and ivories was of very superior quality, Sir William exceeded any other lender in the range and number of his loans. Many of the objects which he lent were amongst the most important of their kind in the exhibition.

His loan of 40 oil paintings, watercolours, drawings and engravings was more numerous than that of any other lender and also possibly superior in artistic interest and variety. Unfortunately this splendid record is somewhat marred by the sale a few years later of three of his most interesting possessions, the two Whistlers, 'The Fur Jacket' (now in the Worcester Art Gallery, Mass., U.S.A.) and the 'Princesse du Pays de la Porcelaine' (now in the Freer Art Gallery, Washington), and Manet's portrait of Victorine Meurent (now in the Museum of Fine Arts, Boston) all of which Burrell had bought from the Scottish art dealer, Alexander Reid about the mid-1890s.

The remainder of Burrell's loans comprised ten works by three living British artists (one by John Lavery, three by Joseph Crawhall, both of whom are linked with the Glasgow School, and six by Phil May), ten by Dutchmen (one by J. Bosboom, seven by Matthew Maris, and two by James Maris), and nine by artists working in Paris (two each by Ribot and Monticelli, and one each by Couture, Daumier, Géricault, Jongkind, and Bargue). One of Crawhall's works was the watercolour of 'The Aviary, Clifton' [62] (called 'The Cockatoo' in the 1901 catalogue) which Burrell acquired soon after it had returned from an extensive exhibition tour of America in 1895. Burrell later formed a very large collection of Crawhall's and May's watercolours and drawings.

The loss of the Whistlers and the Manet is to some extent compensated by a number of pictures lent to the 1901 exhibition by other lenders which were subsequently acquired at various times by Sir William and still form part of the Collection. These include the only other Manet in the exhibition, the pastel now entitled 'Café, Place du Théâtre Français' [49] lent by Arthur Kay who had bought it from Vollard in the Rue Lafitte in the 1890s; two still-lifes of fruit by Courbet, 'The Jetty, Trouville' by Boudin [46], and Bonvin's 'The Spinet' [36]. Cranach's small 'Cupid the Honey Thief complaining to Venus' [9], which was lent by Sir Thomas Gibson Carmichael to hang in one of the Royal Reception Rooms in the exhibition, was acquired by Sir William at or soon after the Carmichael sale in 1902.

Apart from the workshop Velasquez portrait of the 'Infanta Margarita Theresa' (called the 'Infanta Maria Theresa' by Velasquez in the catalogue) and two engravings by Dürer and Cranach, all the pictures which Burrell lent to the exhibition were of the 19th century. There is no reason to think that these loans comprised all he had at the time. The few records which have survived of the pictures sold to Sir William prior to 1901 by Alexander Reid show that in 1899 he bought two paintings by Whistler, 'Nocturne' and 'Paysage', a Raeburn, 'Head of an old Lady', and a Daumier 'Susannah'; none of these was lent to the 1901 exhibition, and only one of them, the probably genuine but somewhat overpainted Daumier, is still in the Collection. Burrell had been buying from Alexander Reid since the 1880s, and all his early purchases, whether bought direct from Reid or not, can probably be attributed to his influence. Reid knew Paris well and after dealing in Barbizon paintings had moved on to the Impressionists. He organised various important exhibitions at his gallery in Glasgow which was known as 'La Société des Beaux Arts'. In 1887 he arranged the first Fantin-Latour exhibition consisting of 35 works straight from the artist's studio. His later exhibitions included Boudin, who was extremely popular in Scotland, and Vuillard. He was handling many of Degas' paintings in the 1890s and about 1901 sold Burrell his first Degas, 'The Girl looking through Field Glasses' [53]. In general Burrell's taste was in sympathy with the underlying trend towards realism in French 19th century painting but his early purchases do not indicate that he was interested in the contemporary work of the Impressionist painters, and apart from Cézanne's 'Château de Médan' [60] Gauguin's 'Breton Girl' [61] and pastels by Degas and Vuillard, he seldom ventured into Post-Impressionism. Many paintings and drawings by 19th century Dutch artists, particularly those by the three Maris brothers, which he had begun to collect by 1900, suggest that he was by no means totally committed to the French School which Reid for the most part was selling (although Reid also sold Dutch paintings), and in fact until 1920 Burrell continued to buy more pictures by Dutch and British artists than by French ones.

The other important part of his collection which Burrell lent to the 1901 exhibition was of tapestries. These included the three Franco-Flemish 16th century tapestries for 'January', 'April', and 'September', forming part of a series of the Months. He also lent a mid-15th century Franco-Burgundian fragment 'The Return from the Campaign' (probably Paris returning with the captive Helen); a long Sheldon cushion cover representing 'Faith, Hope and Charity'; a narrow early 16th century hanging, ascribed to Brussels, called 'The Proposal of Marriage by Proxy'; and seven other pieces which it is impossible to identify. There were also two 'embroidered tapestries' included in Burrell's loans, probably needlework pictures of which he later acquired numerous examples. Burrell did not lend two of his most significant acquisitions, the large and important mid-15th century 'Wine Press', and the later 'Seigneur in his Park' [84]; soon after his collection was further enriched by his purchase of the outstanding Mille Fleurs tapestry, 'Charity overcoming Envy' [91] from Sir Thomas Gibson Carmichael who had lent it to the International Exhibition. Burrell also exhibited seven Persian carpets of which the most remarkable was a 17th century Garden carpet, (under the title of 'Chosroes' Spring' in the 1901 catalogue), which had formerly belonged to Sidney Colvin.

Burrell's loans of pictures and tapestries were far outnumbered by the pieces of furniture and the objects of applied art. Much of the furniture that he provided for one of the Royal Reception Rooms had been borrowed from his family home; the pieces included six Spanish leather chairs, a Gothic chest and a Dutch candelabrum. Elsewhere he showed an English marquetry long case clock, three mirrors, and eleven chairs, variously described as Elizabethan, Dutch, Flemish, Italian, and Cromwellian. He had already acquired some stained glass, and he lent some of the smaller Swiss and Dutch pieces together with three larger Flemish panels of standing saints. Besides this stained glass, which in time became the nucleus of a collection second only to that in the Victoria and Albert Museum, and the antique and the Dutch, Venetian and German 16th and 17th century glass vessels, Burrell exhibited a miscellaneous group of works of bronze, copper, and brass: this included 20 repoussé plates, an aquamanile, two corn measures, a seal die, a doorknocker, a nest of weights, a lamp, a cross, six candlesticks, and a 14th century triple oil stock. There were also some pieces of iron and steel: an iron box, two small padlocks, a lock and plate which represented the 'Lion and the Unicorn' and eight keys. For the most part these still seem to be in the Collection, but the entries for them in the catalogue are usually too brief for positive identification.

The exhibition over, his loans rejoined the works he had not lent to form part of the decoration and furnishings of the house, 8 Great Western Terrace, where he lived after his marriage in 1901. Early photographs of the house's interior are very valuable as a means of establishing what was in Burrell's collection at a time when he was not keeping records, and the 1901 International Exhibition catalogue was not sufficiently detailed to identify many loans beyond those of pictures and tapestries. What is clear, however, is that most of the categories of art which Burrell cultivated were initiated at the turn of the century. A pattern of collecting was established which persisted with remarkable uniformity throughout the remainder of his life.

The problem of knowing what Burrell acquired and when has been largely resolved by the 28 purchase books which he started in 1911. There is no indication whether the earliest entries in the purchase books continue the rhythm of collecting established in the previous years or even represent a lull in Burrell's collecting ardour. If they are the first records of the kind he kept it may be assumed they indicate a new seriousness of purpose, a change from collecting for pleasure to collecting with some distant end in view. Certainly they are an invaluable source of information about his method of collecting and of the astounding scale of his expenditure on works of art. On the average Burrell was spending about £20,000 a year for the 48 years in which he kept records, rising to a first peak in 1936 when he spent nearly £80,000, and a second peak in 1948 when the sum was over £60,000.

In so far as expenditure is concerned, Sir William's purchases during the first few years as recorded in the books were quite modest and chiefly confined to Chinese pottery and bronzes, both of which, contrary to expectation, included many Han, T'ang, Sung as well as the more fashionable later wares. The first recorded picture purchases occur in 1915 when he bought the Dutch 15th century painting, 'The Annunciation' [3], Le Nain's 'Group of Children' [11], the School of Lorraine 'Ecce Homo' [4], together with 23 Chinese ceramics and bronzes and two paintings by Eckhout and La Croce for a total expenditure of £1,172. In general the purchase books show that Burrell was adding to most parts of his collection in varying degrees simultaneously. Although over a limited number of years he tended to be dominated by certain master interests, he was never exclusively so. The Chinese pottery and porcelain, numerically the largest and most wide-ranging part of the Collection, was added to almost every year and included examples of almost every phase of Chinese ceramic production, from the Neolithic to Sung, and later dynasties.

Between 1915 and 1926 the highest sums that Burrell spent each year were almost always for pictures, and it was during this period that he acquired most of the pictures by 19th century masters. In 1926 he purchased Daumier's 'The Miller, his Son and the Ass' [22], Degas' 'The Rehearsal' [54], and Manet's 'At the Café' [48]. From 1927 and onward for an equal period of time, however, pictures were ousted by tapestries, and for many of these he was prepared to pay considerably higher sums than he did for the pictures. In 1927, for example, he bought the large 15th century Franco-Burgundian tapestry entitled 'The Vintages' for £12,600, and on two other occasions he spent five-figure sums on tapestries. In 1937 he spent more on the 15th century tapestry called 'The Betrothal and Marriage' than on either Degas' 'Jockeys in the Rain' or Cezanne's 'Chateau de Médan' bought the same year. The most important additions to the stained glass collection were made in 1938 and 1939.

During the late thirties and forties Burrell's major purchases were often in less predictable fields. In 1939 he bought the set of three James I silver gilt steeple cups [381]; in 1940 the Dietrichstein Persian Flowercarpet; in 1941 the Richard de Bury chest; in 1942 Crawhall's 'The Flowershop'; in 1943 a Chinese Famille Noire vase; in 1944 a Chinese stone seated Lohan [317]; in 1945 an early 16th century Franco-Flemish tapestry of an open-air banquet [87]; in 1946 Rembrandt's 'Self-Portrait' [12]; in 1947 a 15th century Franco-Flemish tapestry from the Alexander set; Burrell's acquisition of Frans Hals' 'Portrait of a Man' [10] for £14,500 in 1948 was the most expensive purchase that he ever made.

From 1947 onward Sir William, who was then in his 86th year, began to explore what was for him an almost totally new field, and most of his purchases during these last ten years of his life were of Egyptian, Greek, Mesopotamian and Persian antiquities. His last major purchase was made in April 1957 when he bought a Urartian bronze head of a bull from Toprak Kale [336]. He also made significant additions to the stained glass including the series of armorial shields from the banqueting hall at Fawsley Hall, Northamptonshire, [101–139], and many pieces from the collection of Lord Rochdale. Another significant purchase, not least because of their influence upon the architects' design of the new buildings for the Burrell Collection, were the large stone portals and windows and the timber screens which Sir William bought from the Hearst Collection in 1954.

In 1927, Burrell, who had been a Trustee of the Tate Gallery and of the National Gallery of Scotland for several years, was knighted for his services to art. In the same year he and Lady Burrell moved to Hutton Castle near Berwick-on-Tweed which he had acquired from Lord Tweedmouth in 1916. During those ten years the castle was being remodelled to receive Burrell's collection as furnishings, and some of the works were built into the fabric of the rooms. But as the Collection continued to grow it exceeded the accommodation available, and for many years much of it was widely dispersed on loan to art galleries, museums, and cathedrals in England, Scotland, and Wales.

Like many wealthy men, Burrell was of reserved character, and in the midst of the beautiful objects which filled his home he led a comparatively frugal existence. Starting as a private collector, he became during 30 years or more, a collector for posterity rather than for himself. He always preserved a keen intellectual and artistic interest in his collection about which he had read widely and for the details of which he had an excellent memory. By nature he was clearly attracted by vigour of form and colour rather than by elegance, and as a consequence the Collection is rich in works of the 15th, 16th, and 17th centuries but deficient in those of the 18th century. The Collection is probably one of the largest ever assembled by one man. Certainly the largest ever given to one city.

Catalogue

An asterisk after the title of a work denotes that the work, or detail, is illustrated.

The measurements of each work are given with height followed by width.

The Burrell Collection registration number of each work is given in brackets after its size.

Paintings

Domenico Veneziano (active 1438–61)
1 The Judgement of Paris*
Wood, 15⅛ × 19⅝in. (35.634)
One of four cassone panels attributed by
Schubring (*Cassoni*, 1915, nos.165, 166,
167 and 169) to the Paris Master. The
attribution to Domenico Veneziano was
first suggested by Salmi (*Uccello, Castagno,
Veneziano*, 1938, pp.85–6, 175–6) but more
recently opinion has veered in the direction
of Pesellino. Exhibited: 'The Art of
Painting in Florence and Siena',
Wildenstein's Gallery, London, 1965, no.53.
From the Bonaffé, Gibson Carmichael and
Benson Collections; acquired by Sir
William in 1936.

Giovanni Bellini (active c.1459–1516)
2 Virgin and Child*
Wood, 24½ × 18¾in. (35.4)
One of six closely related madonnas dated
by Berenson (*Venetian Pictures*, I, 1957,
p.31) to the years 1488–90. Exhibited:
'Primitives to Picasso', R.A., London, 1962,
no.36. In the Palazzo Barberini until
after 1930; acquired by Sir William in
1936.

Master of the Brunswick Diptych (active
1485–1500)
3 The Annunciation*
Wood, 17½ × 14in. (35.639)
One of three surviving panels from an
altar-piece of c.1485–90 dedicated to the
Virgin by a master active at Haarlem who
was a close follower of Geertgen tot Sint
Jans to whom his works are sometimes
attributed. The diptych from which he
derives his pseudonym is in the Herzog
Anton-Ulrich Museum in Brunswick.
Exhibited: 'Primitives to Picasso', R.A.,
London, 1962, no.19. From the C. T.
Crews and Martin Collections; acquired
by Sir William in 1915.

School of Lorraine (c.1470)
4 Ecce Homo*
Wood, 21¾ × 15½in. (35.300)
Acquired by Sir William in 1915 from the
C.T. Crews Collection with the above
attribution. In volume 5 of *Die
Altniederländische Malerei* (1927, p.73 and
p.139) M. J. Friedländer lists it together
with an almost identical version on the art
market in Rome as the work of the Master
of the Virgo inter Virgines (active 1470–90)
whose style has a superficial resemblance to
that of Hieronymus Bosch.

Hans Memlinc (c.1433–94)
5 The Virgin of the Annunciation*
Wood, 23 × 14in. (35.533)
This panel, originally of the same size as
no.6 and from the same altar-piece, was
formerly in the Wynn Ellis, Leonard Gow
and H. Weise Collections; it was acquired
by Sir William in 1948. Other panels from
the altar-piece represent 'The Nativity'
(Manchester Art Gallery), 'The
Adoration of the Magi' (Prado, Madrid)
and 'The Presentation in the Temple'
(National Gallery, Washington). The
overpainted hand of the angel of the
Annunciation can still be dimly discerned.

Hans Memlinc
6 Flight into Egypt
Wood, 23½ × 20½in. (35.532)
See no.5. First associated with an
altar-piece reconstructed by Hulin de Loo
(*Burlington Magazine*, LII, 1928, pp.160 ff)
by Friedländer (*Die Altniederländische
Malerei*, VI, 1928, pp.21, 122, no.32).
Exhibited: 'Primitives to Picasso', R.A.,
London, 1962, no.21. Formerly in the
Schiff Collection (sold Paris, 1905);
acquired by Sir William in 1936. The
horseman in the cornfield is probably
Herod's emissary who according to legend
was sent in search of the Holy Family and
was deceived by the harvesters.

Jan de Gossaert (Mabuse) (1472–1533)
7 Virgin and Child
Wood, 28 × 22in. (35.303)
Dated 1529. After a picture by Joos van
Cleve of which there are numerous
versions, sometimes in reverse. Acquired
1916.

Lucas Cranach the Elder (1472–1553)
8 A Stag Hunt
Wood, 32¾ × 47in. (35.73)
Signed with the winged serpent device and
dated 1529 on the tree bottom centre.
Other versions are at Vienna, Copenhagen
and Basle, the Vienna picture probably
being the prototype. The huntsmen in the
foreground have been identified by
Friedländer and Rosenberg (*Die Gemälde
von Lucas Cranach*, 1932, p.71) as the
Elector Frederick the Wise of Saxony, the
Emperor Maximilian I and the Elector
John the Constant of Saxony. The last
named is presumed to have been with
the picture in memory of the event after
the death of the Elector Frederick and the
Emperor. Exhibited at Manchester in 1961
('German Art 1400–1800', no.85). The
picture is recorded as having been with
Lawrie and Co., Glasgow, for 1899–1905
and was probably acquired by Sir William
soon after.

Lucas Cranach the Elder
**9 Cupid the Honey Thief complaining
to Venus***
Wood, 20¼ × 14½in. (35.74)
Signed with the winged device and dated:
1545. 'While the boy cupid plunders
honey from the beehive, the bee fastens
on his finger with piercing sting; so in like
manner the brief and fleeting pleasure
which we seek injures us with sad pain.'
The Latin inscription of which this is a
translation is from an idyll traditionally
ascribed to Theocritus. There are a
number of variants at Copenhagen (dated

1530) and elsewhere. Exhibited at Manchester in 1961 ('German Art 1400–1800', no.87). It was lent to the Glasgow International Exhibition, 1901 (cat. p.106) by Sir Thomas Gibson Carmichael, Bart. who sold it the following year either directly or indirectly to Sir William.

Frans Hals (1581/5–1666)
10 Portrait of a Man
Canvas, 46 × 36in. (35.276)
This portrait, formerly the property of the Coleborne family, achieved considerable notoriety on 16 March 1937 when it was acquired for a large sum by a dealer at a sale in Nonsuch Park. It was included, as a work of c.1639, in the Frans Hals exhibition in Haarlem later the same year (cat. no.79). It was acquired by Sir William in 1948.

Antoine Le Nain (1588–1648)
11 Group of Children
Copper, 8½ × 11in. (35.578)
According to Collins Baker (*Apollo*, VIII, 1928, p.67) probably the work of Antoine who is said in a history of Laon, the brothers' birth-place, published in 1711 to have specialised in miniatures and little portraits. G. Isarlo (*La Renaissance*, XXI, 1938, pp.1–58) ascribes the small paintings of children on wood or copper to the period 1630–40. Acquired by Sir William in 1915 at the C. T. Crews Sale. In 1927 he bought 'nearly a duplicate' from the W. A. Coats Collection (cat. 1904, pl.81) which he gave to Berwick-on-Tweed in 1949.

Rembrandt van Rijn (1606–69)
12 Portrait of the Artist
Wood, 24¾ × 18½in. (oval) (35.600)
Signed and dated: RHL van Rijn 1632 (RHL in monogram). One of the earliest self-portraits painted in Amsterdam where he had moved from Leiden in 1631. The picture was owned by the Regent of France, duc d'Orléans, in 1727, and came to England in 1792 when the Flemish and Dutch pictures were sold by Philippe Egalité. It was sold by Lord Leconfield in

1927 and acquired by Sir William at the Viscount Rothermere Sale in 1946. Various copies are listed by Hofstede de Groot (*Catalogue of Dutch Painters*, VI, 1916). Exhibited: 'Primitives to Picasso', R.A., London, 1962, no.124.

J. B. Oudry (1686–1755)
13 The Dog
Canvas, 35½ × 44½in. (35.585)
Signed and dated: J.B. Oudry 1751. Possibly the picture exhibited at the Salon of 1751 described as: 'Un devant de Cheminée representant un chien avec une jatte auprès de lui' in the opinion of Sir Francis Watson rather than the larger unsigned version in the Musée de la Vénerie at Senlis, with which the entry has hitherto been associated. The Burrell picture has been reduced in size. Acquired by 1924 when Sir William lent it to the Tate Gallery, London.

J. A. D. Ingres (1780–1867)
14 Portrait of Tylman Suys
Pencil on paper, 8½ × 5¾in. (35.287)
Signed and dated: Rome 1818. Tieleman Franciscus Suys (1783–1861) was in the 19th century the leading neo-classical architect of Belgium and Holland. The drawing was lent in 1913 by Mme L. Laureys to an exhibition at the Palais des Beaux-Arts, Paris (cat. no.342); it was acquired by Sir William in 1923.

J. L. A. T. Géricault (1791–1824)
15 Two Brown Horses
Wood, 12⅞ × 12⅝in. (35.265)
Inscribed with the names of the horses on the horizontal bar of the hay-loft: 'L'inconnu' and 'L'amicale'. As a young man, probably beginning in 1810, Géricault, while staying with his uncle, M. Caruel, near Versailles, used to visit the imperial stables. Acquired, with the following, in 1926.

J. L. A. T. Géricault
16 The Grey Horse
Wood, 12⅞ × 9⅞in. (35.273)
The head reinforced with the same bold

strokes of the wood tip of the brush that were used to inscribe the name Telemaque. Acquired 1926.

J. L. A. T. Géricault
17 Prancing Grey Horse
Canvas, 17¾ × 21½in. (35.271)
Described by Clément (*Gércault, Étude Biographique et Critique*, 1879, no.48), as a study for the Charging Chasseur in the Louvre, the artist's first major production which was exhibited in the Salon of 1812. It was bought at the Géricault studio sale of 1824 by Léon Cogniet whose name is inscribed on the stretcher together with the words 'par Géricault'. It was later in the W.A. Coats Collection (cat. 1904, pl.69) and was acquired by Sir William in 1935.

J. L. A. T. Géricault
18 The Polish Trumpeter*
Canvas, 16 × 13in. (35.270)
Recorded by Clément (1879, no.22) as 'La Trompette de Lanciers polonais sur un cheval blanc'. It corresponds closely with the description which he gives of a lost picture (no.57) thought to represent the death in 1813 of Prince Joseph Poniatowski, whom Napoleon had made commander of the Polish legion. A very similar equestrian portrait of slightly larger dimensions by Géricault representing another commander of the Polish Legion, General Wincenty Krasinki, is in the National Museum, Warsaw. Formerly in the Collot (sold 1852, no.39) and James Nathaniel de Rothschild Collections; acquired by Sir William in 1929.

J. B. C. Corot (1796–1875)
19 Peasant's House at Fontainebleau
Canvas, 22 × 18¼in. (35.61)
Signed: Corot. Painted 1860–70 (see Robaut, *L'Œuvre de Corot*, III, Paris, 1905, no.1316). Acquired by Sir William in 1922. Shown in Marlborough New London Gallery, 1963, no.33.

J. B. C. Corot
20   Portrait of a Woman
Canvas, 17½ × 10¼in. (35.62)
Signed: Corot. Painted 1850–5 (see Robaut,
L'Œuvre de Corot, II, Paris, 1905, no.661).
Given by Corot to his friend Grisart; later
in the Charles de Tournemine Collection
(sold Paris, 15 April 1880, no.16); acquired
by Sir William by 1924 when he lent it to
the Tate Gallery exhibition of Burrell
pictures (no.52). Shown in Marlborough
New London Gallery, 1963, no.20.

F. V. E. Delacroix (1798–1863)
21   The White Horse
Canvas, 18 × 22in. (35.250)
Painted about 1823 in emulation of
Géricault. According to Robaut (*L'Œuvre
Complet*, Paris, 1885, no.75) Delacroix
treasured this study which hung in his
dining-room. It was bought at the
Delacroix Sale (no.202) by M. Verde
Delisle, a friend of Delacroix, by whose
grandson it was sold in 1931 (see
C. Thompson, *Scottish Arts Review*, VI,
no.3, p.12). Acquired by Sir William in
1931 from Dieterle.

H. Daumier (1808–1879)
22   The Miller, his Son and the Ass*
Canvas, 52 × 38½in. (35.222)
Signed: h. Daumier. Painted expressly
for the Salon where it was exhibited in
1849 (no.484). The three women, perhaps
inspired by Rubens, appear without the
riding miller and his son in a picture of
equal size called 'Les Ribaudes' (K. E.
Maison, *Honoré Daumier*, 1968, I, no.22)
and a much smaller version of the
whole composition is in a private collection
in Zurich (Maison, I, no.23). Formerly in
the collection of Col. Woods; acquired by
Sir William in 1926.

H. Daumier
23   Don Quixote and Sancho Panza
Canvas, 12¾ × 9½in. (35.217)
Signed: h. D. Painted 1864/5 according
to Maison (I, no.17) who records another
version of similar date in New York (I,
no.172) and a pastiche in France (E. Fuchs,

Der Maler Daumier, 1930, no.304a). The
picture of this title lent by Sir William to
the Glasgow International Exhibition of
1901 (no.1342) was sold the following
year and is now in Chicago. He acquired
this picture in 1922.

H. Daumier
24   The Good Samaritan
Canvas, 57½ × 45in. (35.215)
Signed: h. Daumier. Possibly painted
about 1850–60 but most authorities agree
that it must have been finished after
Daumier's death (Maison, II, no.1). Date
of acquisition unrecorded but by 1924
when Sir William lent it to the Tate
exhibition of paintings from the Burrell
Collection (no.55).

H. Daumier
25   The Heavy Burden
Canvas, 15½ × 12¼in. (35.213)
Signed: h. Daumier. Painted 1855/6
according to Maison (I, no.85) who records
another very closely related version in a
London private collection (I, no.86) and a
much larger one, probably painted three
to four years later, in Paris (I, no.121). The
laundress and child form the subject of a
terracotta sculpture by Daumier in
the Walters Art Gallery, Baltimore
(Gobin, *Daumier Sculpteur*, 1952, pl.30).
Acquired by Sir William by 1901 when
he lent it to the Glasgow International
Exhibition (no.1411).

H. Daumier
26   The Bathers*
Wood, 10 × 12⅝in. (35.212)
Painted 1846/8 according to Maison (I,
no.17) who relates it to two other paintings
(I, nos.15 and 16) and a crayon and
watercolour compositional study of
unknown location (D 250). Acquired by
Sir William at the sale of the Leonard Gow
Collection in 1936.

H. Daumier
27   The Print Collector
Canvas, 14 × 10in. (35.210)
Signed: h. D. Painted 1860/3 according to
Maison (I, no.151) who considers it to be

probably the first of two closely related
versions of which the other (I, no.152) is
in the Art Institute, Chicago. Acquired by
Sir William from Barbizon House in 1923.

H. Daumier
28   La Parade
Crayon, pencil and wash, 16 × 11⅝in.
(35.224)
Inscribed: 'à mon ami Jules Dupré' and
signed: h. D. There are several variations
on the theme among Daumier's drawings
of which the closest in size, technique and
composition is in a private collection in
Paris (Maison, II, nos.533 and 534).
Acquired in 1924 from Barbizon House by
Sir William who lent it to the exhibition
of French Art at Burlington House in
1932 (no.922).

H. Daumier
29   A Street Musician
Pen and wash, 11¼ × 8½in. (35.223)
An almost exact repetition of this drawing
(Maison, II, no.334) is in a German private
collection (Maison, II, no.333). Acquired
by Sir William from Reid and Lefevre in
1927. There are 18 works by Daumier in
the Collection.

J. F. Millet (1814–75)
30   The Shepherdess
Wood, 11¾ × 6½in. (35.544)
Signed: J. F. Millet and J. F. M.; inscribed
on the back '25 avril, 1849 Jean François
Millet'. A black chalk study is in the
Fitzwilliam Museum (Louis C. G. Clarke
bequest), Cambridge. Formerly in the
W. A. Coats Collection (cat. 1904, pl.84);
acquired by Sir William from Reid and
Lefevre in 1935.

J. F. Millet
31   A Peasant Family
Chalk on canvas on wood, 24 × 17 in.
(35.539)
A study for the oil in the National
Gallery of Wales, Cardiff, one of Millet's
last works which remained unfinished in
his studio. There are a number of other
studies in the Louvre. Acquired by Sir
William in 1917 from Alexander Reid.

J. F. Millet
32 The Wool Carder*
Chalk, 14 × 10in. (35.536)
Stamped with initials: J. F. M. Dated by
R. L. Herbert (Yale University) to
c.1848; not a study for Millet's paintings
of 1863 called 'La Cardeuse'. A possibly
identical drawing of the same name by
Millet was lent by T. G. Arthur to the
Glasgow International Exhibition, 1901,
p.162, no.335. Acquired by Sir William
in 1923. There are 11 works by Millet in
the Collection.

T. Couture (1815–79)
33 Le Conventionnel
Canvas, 26¼ × 22¼in. (35.70)
Signed: T. C. A study for one of the
figures in Couture's unfinished picture
'Les Enrôlements des Volontaires de
1792', commissioned after the revolution
of 1848. Another version is in the Boston
Museum of Fine Arts. Lent by Sir William
to the International Exhibition, Glasgow,
1901, no.1285.

C. F. Daubigny (1817–78)
34 Landscape with Mill
Wood, 12 × 20⅜in. (35.209)
Signed and dated 1872. Acquired 1937.

F. S. Bonvin (1817–87)
35 The Crow*
Wood, 16½ × 19½in. (35.8)
Signed and dated: F. B. '49. One of the
earliest of the 13 works by Bonvin in the
Collection when he was evolving a style of
still-life painting modelled on a study of
Chardin. Acquired by 1924 when
Sir William lent it to the Tate Gallery.

F. S. Bonvin
36 The Spinet
Canvas, 17¼ × 13¼in. (35.10)
Signed and dated: F. Bonvin 1862.
Reflects Bonvin's study of the Dutch
masters of the 17th century, particularly
Terborch and de Hooch. Lent to the
Glasgow International Exhibition 1901
(no.1258) by Mrs. A. J. Kirkpatrick and
bought by Sir William at the Kirkpatrick
Sale (Glasgow, 1 April 1914, lot 291).

J. D. G. Courbet (1819–77)
37 Charity of a Beggar at Ornans
Canvas, 83 × 69in. (35.64)
Signed and dated: 68 Gustave Courbet.
The last of Courbet's large social-realist
pictures in his 'sur la grande route' series
of which 'The Stonebreakers' painted in
1850 was the first. A contemporary
caricature by Alfred Darjon (L'Eclipse,
24 May 1868) in which the beggar is
transformed into a scarecrow was
occasioned by its exhibition in the Salon of
1868 (no.608). Acquired 1923.

J. D. G. Courbet
38 Portrait of Mlle. Aubé de la Holde*
Canvas, 36¼ × 29in. (35.65)
Painted at Trouville in September 1865.
Courbet refers to it in a letter dated 16
September, to Urbain Cuenot at Ornans:
'. . . the casino has given me a superb
apartment overlooking the sea, and there
I do the portraits of the prettiest ladies in
Trouville . . . At the moment I am doing
that of Mlle Haubé de la Holde, a young
Parisian, in her own way as beautiful as
Mlle. Karoly'. The portrait was shown in
Courbet's exhibition of his own work in
Paris in 1867. Acquired by Sir William
from Alexander Reid in 1920.

J. D. G. Courbet
39 The Washer Women*
Canvas, 8 × 11in. (35.69)
The setting is reminiscent of Courbet's
native village Ornans, in the Franche
Comté, which is built on either side of the
river Loue. It was lent to the Glasgow
International Exhibition of 1888 by
Mrs. A. J. Kirkpatrick and acquired by
Sir William at the Kirkpatrick Sale
(Glasgow, 1 April 1914, lot 290).

J. D. G. Courbet
40 Iris and Gillyflowers
Canvas, 16 × 8½in. (35.68)
Signed: G. C. Inscribed on the back:
'Picture given by Courbet to Jules Dupré,
the great French landscape painter.'
Acquired by Sir William in 1923.

J. B. Jongkind (1819–91)
41 Fabrique de Cuirs Forts*
Canvas, 13½ × 16⅜in. (35.293)
Signed and dated: Jongkind Jeudi (?)
7 avril 1868 (or Paris (?) 17 avril 1868).

Another version (dated 19 April 1868) is in
the Gemeente-museum, The Hague; a
third (signed and dated 1873) was exhibited
in the Jongkind exhibition at the Galerie
Schmit in Paris, May–June 1966, no.48
with the title: 'Paris, Démolition de la
rue des Francs-Bourgeois'. Acquired by
1901 when Sir William lent it to the
Glasgow International Exhibition (cat.
p.99, no.1405, 'Street in Paris').

A. T. Ribot (1823–91)
42 The Cooks*
Canvas, 29 × 24in. (35.607)
Signed and dated: t. Ribot 1862. This
picture, also called 'Les Plumeurs', was
exhibited in the Salon of 1863. A
water-colour sketch (7½ × 5½in.) figuring
the seated cook on the right belonging to
Sir Frederick Wedmore was sold at
Sotheby's, 1 March 1973 lot 115. Acquired
by Sir William in 1922.

A. T. Ribot
43 Mother and Daughter
Canvas, 18½ × 15¼in. (35.610)
Signed: t. Ribot. Date of acquisition
unrecorded but by 1923 when it is
mentioned in The Studio (15 February
1923, p.64) as being among the Burrell
pictures on loan to the National Gallery
of Scotland. There are nine works by
Ribot in the Collection.

A. J. T. Monticelli (1824–86)
44 The New Vintage
Wood, 16 × 23½in. (35.558)
Formerly in the W. A. Coats Collection
(cat. 1904, pl.91); acquired by Sir William
at the Coats Sale, London, 1927. The
Collection contains 14 pictures by
Monticelli.

A. J. T. Monticelli
45 The Bazaar Marseilles
Wood, 14¾ × 23¾in. (35.549)
Signed: A. Monticelli. Lent to the
Glasgow International Exhibition, 1901
(no.1314) by Sir William who later sold it
to the uncle of Mrs. Winifred Glen-Coats
Parsons from whose collection he rebought
it at Christie's in 1942. The reverse bears
a painting of children by Monticelli.

L. E. Boudin (1824–98)
46 The Jetty at Trouville
Canvas, 25½ × 36½in. (35.43)
Signed: Eugene Boudin 69; and inscribed
'Trouville'. Lent to the Glasgow
International Exhibition 1901 (no.1420)
by Major Thorburn, Peebles. Returned to
Scotland in 1912 when it was bought by
J. Tattersal, Dundee, at the G.N. Stevens
Sale (Christie's 14 June 1912, no.96).
Acquired by Sir William from Alexander
Reid in 1919. Schmit, *Eugène Boudin*, I,
1973, no.492.

L. E. Boudin
**47 The Beach at Trouville: the
Empress Eugénie**
Wood, 13½ × 22½in. (35.45)
Signed: E. Boudin 63. The Empress,
preceded by two promenading ladies and
followed by three more, is in the central
group wearing white; the occasion may
have been the opening of a new casino in
1863. The picture (see Schmit, I, 1973,
no.280) was sold at the Hôtel Drouot,
Paris, 5 March 1923, no.15; it was
acquired by Sir William in April 1923.
There are 11 works by Boudin in the
Collection.

E. Manet (1832–1883)
48 At the Café*
Pastel on linen, 24 × 20in. (35.305)
Signed: Manet. This pastel of about 1878,
showing two ladies drinking iced beer in
the Cabaret Reichshoffen in the boulevard
Rochechouart was shown by Manet in his
exhibition at the Vie Moderne, Paris, in
1880. 'Les bockeuses', as it was called, was
bought by a Dutchman and was later in

the collection of Paul Rosenberg; acquired
by Sir William in 1926 from Alexander
Reid.

E. Manet
49 Café, Place du Théâtre Français*
Pastel on canvas, 12¾ × 18in. (35.306)
Signed: Manet. In his book (*Treasure
Trove in Art*, 1939, p.306) the Scottish
collector, Arthur Kay, describes how he
bought this pastel (called 'Folies Bergères'
at the time) from Vollard's modest premises
in the rue Lafitte in the nineties.
Subsequently it was returned to France
before being acquired by Sir William
in 1923, as 'Au Moulin Rouge'. It has also
been erroneously called 'Café, Place du
Palais-Royal', as Tabarant notes in the
1947 edition of his book on Manet (p.431).

E. Manet
50 The Ham
Canvas, 12¾ × 16¼in. (35.308)
Signed: Manet. Painted about 1880
at Bellevue, it was first shown in the
posthumous Manet exhibition in the
École des Beaux-Arts in 1884 (no.97). At
the Pertuiset Sale in 1888 it was acquired
by Degas who hung it in his bedroom in
the rue Victor Massé in Montmartre
beside his portrait of Manet listening to
Mme Manet at the piano. It was sold in
the Degas sale of 1918 (no.75) and was
later acquired by the Scottish collector,
Leonard Gow, before its purchase by
Sir William in 1936.

E. Manet
51 Marie Colombier*
Pastel on canvas, 22 × 14in. (35.309)
Signed: Manet. Marie Colombier, actress
and later hostess of renown, visited
Manet's studio at Bellevue in January–
February 1880 and was delighted with her
portrait, as both her own and Jules
Claretie's letter of 16 February indicate
(Tabarant, 1947, p.397). It was included in
the Manet posthumous exhibition of 1884
(no.139) and was later in the A. A. Pellerin
Collection. It was acquired by Sir William
from Bernheim-Jeune in 1922.

E. Manet
52 Roses in a Champagne Glass
Canvas, 12¾ × 9¾in. (35.310)
Signed: Manet. Painted in 1882 when
Manet was semi-invalid. Its first owner
was the lively actress, Mery Laurent, to
whom Manet had probably given it in
recognition of the many gifts of flowers
and sweets he had received from her. Its
first Scottish owner was Leonard Gow
from whom it passed to Sir William by
purchase in 1937. There are nine works by
Manet in the Collection.

H. G. E. Degas (1834–1917)
53 Girl looking through Field Glasses*
Oil on paper on canvas, 12½ × 7½in. (35.239)
Previously known as 'Girl looking through
opera glasses', it was revealed as a study
for 'Aux Courses, les Jockeys' when the
latter (now in a private collection in
London) was cleaned at the National
Gallery in 1960 (*Burlington Magazine*,
December 1960, p.536). There are various
related studies, one of which in a Swiss
private collection is inscribed 'Lyda'
probably indicating that the model was
Lydia Cassatt (*Apollo*, February, 1972,
pp.129–34). It was the first work by Degas
to be acquired by Sir William who bought
it from Alexander Reid at the turn of the
century and soon after included it in a sale
of Burrell pictures at Christie's (14 June,
1902, lot 8, bought in).

H. G. E. Degas
54 The Rehearsal*
Canvas, 23 × 33in. (35.246)
Signed: Degas. Dated by Lemoisne (*Degas
et son Œuvre*, 1946–9, no.430) to 1877 but
possibly earlier if this is the picture seen by
Edmond de Goncourt in the artist's studio
on 13 February 1874. A related but distinct
picture in the Corcoran Gallery,
Washington, repeats the motive of the
spiral staircase on the left and the group
in the right foreground with variations.
The original title seems to have been
'Foyer de la danse' and it was as such that
Theo van Gogh bought it on behalf of

Boussod and Valadon on 12 October 1888 from Georges Petit for 5,220 francs and sold it on 29 November 1888 to Émile Blanche for 8,000 francs (*Gazette des Beaux-Arts*, January–February, 1973, p.28). Acquired by Sir William per Alexander Reid and Lefevre in 1926.

H. G. E. Degas
55   Portrait of Émile Duranty*
Tempera, water-colour and pastel on linen, 39¾ × 39½in. (35.232)
Signed and dated: Degas 1879. The portrait, for which there is a preliminary and smaller version in the Adolph Lewison Collection, New York, was included in the catalogue of the 4th Impressionist exhibition of 1879 but not shown (being unfinished by 10 April) until the following year when it appeared in the 5th exhibition after Duranty's death on 9 April 1880. It was sold in the 1st sale of the Degas studio (7–8 May 1918, no.48) and was acquired by Sir William in 1923 from L.H. Lefevre and Son. It exemplifies the conception of portraiture as a portrayal of the man in his normal surroundings propounded by the critic and novelist, Louis-Émile-Edmond Duranty (1833–80).

H. G. E. Degas
56   Lady with Parasol*
Canvas, 10¾ × 8in. (35.234)
Signed: Degas. Ascribed by Lemoisne (vol. III, p.537, no.920) to the period 1887–90. Formerly in the Manzi, Denys Cochon and Jules Strauss Collection in Paris; acquired by Sir William from Alexander Reid and Lefevre in 1927.

H. Fantin-Latour (1836–1904)
57   Chrysanthemums
Canvas, 21¾ × 25½in. (35.260)
Signed and dated: Fantin 1874. Belonged to Edwin Edwards, the artist's chief friend and patron in England; later in the Laurent Collection (sold Paris, 21 February 1913, no.22). Acquired by Sir William in 1917 from Alexander Reid.

H. Fantin-Latour
58   Spring Flowers*
Canvas, 11½ × 9½in. (35.261)
Signed and dated: Fantin '78. Belonged to Edwin Edwards and to William Sutch in London. Acquired by Sir William in 1923 from Tempelaere.

A. Sisley (1839–1899)
59   The Bell Tower, Noisy-le-Roi: Autumn*
Canvas, 18 × 24in. (35.625)
Signed and dated: Sisley 74. Almost certainly painted in October, soon after Sisley's return to France from Hampton Court, the view shows the small village of Noisy-le-Roi, a short distance from Louveciennes and Marly-le-Roi (see catalogue of Sisley exhibition, Nottingham Art Gallery, February 1971, no.3). Formerly in the A. Dachery Collection from which it was acquired by Baronne Henri de Rothschild in 1899. Acquired by Sir William from George Petit, Paris, in 1929.

P. Cézanne (1839–1906)
60   Le Château de Médan*
Canvas, 23¼ × 28½in. (35.53)
Signed: P. Cézanne. Painted from an island in the Seine opposite Zola's property, which included the château de Médan as well as his own house (out of sight to the right) probably during Cézanne's visit to Médan in the summer of 1880, when his execution was marked by dense layers of paint applied in parallel brush strokes, diagonally for the trees and vegetation and horizontally for the water. It was acquired, perhaps from Père Tanguy, by Gauguin who took it with him to Denmark in 1884 and wrote a glowing description of it in his recollections published in 1903. After its sale by Gauguin's wife, Mette, it was in various collections before its acquisition in New York through T. J. Honeyman for Reid and Lefevre from whom Sir William acquired it in 1937.

P. Gauguin (1848–1903)
61   Breton Girl*
Chalk, 18⅛ × 12½in. (35.264)
A study for a figure in the painting 'Four Breton Women Talking', now in the Bäyerische Staatsgemäldesammlung, Munich, which is signed and dated 1886 (see catalogue of 'Gauguin and the Pont-Aven Group', Arts Council, 1966, no.43). Acquired by Sir William in 1936, from Knoedler.

J. Crawhall (1861–1913)
62   The Aviary, Clifton
Water-colour, 20 × 14in. (35.77)
Signed and dated: J. Crawhall Jnr. Clifton '88. This water-colour was Crawhall's most successful production as a young man. It was first exhibited at Messrs Paterson & Thomas's in Glasgow 1888. In 1890 it was shown in Munich with other works of the Glasgow school and was awarded a second-class gold medal. In 1895 it was shown extensively in the U.S.A. and was probably acquired soon after its return to Scotland by Sir William who lent it to the Glasgow International Exhibition in 1901 (no.695, 'The Cockatoo'). It is reproduced in colour as a frontispiece in Adrian Bury's book on Joseph Crawhall (1958).

J. Crawhall
63   The Governess Cart
Gouache on linen, 12 × 14¾in. (35.129)
Signed: J. Crawhall. Acquired in 1933 from Alexander Reid and Lefevre. There are 132 works by Crawhall in the Collection.

Tapestries

German, Swiss

German Tapestry Fragment
64 Dorsal with birds and beasts
Wool, 1ft.9½in. × 1ft.8in. (46.1)
This fragment (Kurth, *Die Deutschen Bildteppiche des Mittelalters*, 1, 1925, pp.166 and 258) may be from a longer strip in the Museum at Freiburg-im-Breisgau showing a similar repeating pattern of interlacing lozenges filled alternately with a pair of addorsed birds and a monster on variously coloured grounds. In the spaces between are foliated rosettes alternating with ivy-leaves. The Freiburg panel has, in addition, a border top and bottom, embellished with early gothic initials, flowers and tiny beasts. The bird motives are taken from Arabic silk-woven textiles of the 13th century. In two 15th-century pictures with scenes from the life of St. Clara attributed to Wolf Katzheimer in the picture gallery at Bamberg, two tapestries of similar pattern are depicted, one as a hanging beside the altar, and the other as a carpet on which St. Clara kneels in front of the altar. The Freiburg strip may have come from the Dominican convent of Adelhausen. Formerly in the collection of Dr. R. Forrer, Strassburg, and later of Dr. Albert Figdor, Vienna, and Fritz Iklé from whom it was acquired by Sir William in 1933.

German Tapestry Fragment
65 Three Prophets*
Wool, 2ft.1in. × 4ft.1in. (46.3)
Probably woven in Franconia (? Nuremberg) during the first quarter of the 15th century (Kurth, 1, pp.168 and 258) as part of a longer frieze of prophets debating in pairs. It has been shown by Fraulein Barbara Leisner, Munich, that the inscriptions are taken from the books of proverbs such as the *Frei Dank*. In this fragment the first is partly illegible owing to faulty repairs. The second reads:

'Got · und · mensch · in natur / ist · wol · ein · wirdiklich · figur.' ('God and man in nature is certainly a true proposition') and the third: 'Kein · grosser · wu(n)der · ny · gescha / den · da · man · got · in · menscheit · sach' ('No greater miracle ever happened than when man saw God in mankind'). Formerly in the Collection of Dr. List, Vienna. Acquired by Sir William in 1930.

South German Tapestry
66 Holy Trinity with the Arma Christi*
Wool and linen, 3ft.4ft. (46.10)
Part of an altar-hanging (Kurth, 1, pp.176 and 263) probably woven in Nuremberg c.1420 showing, in a dark blue background, the Trinity, with Christ represented as the Man of Sorrows between the kneeling figures of the Virgin and St. John (now seen respectively to the right and left of Christ owing to the fact that the tapestry has been reversed and is now shown from the back). On either side stand angels with the instruments, banner, and arms of the Passion. A portion (formerly in the Figdor Collection, now at Castagnola near Lausanne) from the left side bearing part of the missing wings of the angel, shows a kneeling donor, and the arms of the Count of Schwarzburg. Dr. Léonie von Wilckens (*Anzeiger des Germanisches National-museums*, 1973, pp.74–5, fig.22) compares this impressive work with the best paintings in Vatican MS. cod. pal. lat. 1066 and points out that it was never in the Stieglitz Collection, Petersburg, as Dr. Kurth stated. Formerly in the Collections of Hermann Sax, Vienna, Heckscher, Sir Hercules Read, Major Sir Humphrey Noble. Acquired by Sir William in 1946.

German Tapestry Altar-Frontal
67 The Adoration of the Magi
Wool and silk, 3ft. × 6ft. (46.5)
While the oldest of the three kings, wearing an oak-leaf patterned robe, kneels with his gift of golden coins, two angels bearing an imperial crown hover above the Virgin's head, and from the star in the east, rays descend towards the child's head. The scene is watched by the wistful figure of St. Joseph from behind a brick wall, and the two younger kings, both sumptuously clad, stand by with gifts. On the left stands St. Erasmus holding a windlass and on the right St. Dorothy with a basket of flowers. The donor, Erasmus Schürstab, kneels to the left with his coat of arms (argent, two bands in saltire gules, surmounted by the bust of a Negro bishop as crest) and his seven sons. His first wife Dorothea Hallerin, with her armorial shield, kneels with her six daughters including the eldest, a nun, and one married daughter (denoted by a shield with four quarterings). In the centre kneels the donor's second wife, Ursula Pfinzig, with her armorial achievements. This antependium (Kurth, 1, pp. 182 and 269) was probably woven in the nunnery of the Holy Sepulchre at Bamberg, where Schürstab's eldest daughter was a nun between 1472 and 1480. Acquired by Sir William in 1933.

German Tapestry with Wildmen
68 Haymaking*
Wool and linen, 3ft.1in. × 5ft. (46.26)
Probably woven in Alsace, c.1400–25 (Kurth, vol. 1, pp.126 and 233). On a dark blue patterned ground, wild men and women and one woman in ordinary peasant dress are engaged in scything, and in spreading and piling hay with rakes. To the right on a slightly higher plane, a woman wearing a daisy-patterned robe, holding a banner bearing a rake as an ensign, personifies the hay-harvest month of July, as the scroll, which partly surrounds her shows: 'der · howat · bin · ich · gena(n)t'. Beneath the harvesters, a lower zone is patterned with hoop-like mounds each filled with a plant. Among them are sprites riding hobby-horses with

wind-vanes (seemingly of the same genre that appear in some of the large 15th/16th century Franco-Flemish tapestries e.g. no. 84 in this exhibition), playing musical instruments, and picking flowers. The numerous boldly flowing scrolls are inscribed in an Alemanian dialect with Alsatian peculiarities. It may have formed part of a series illustrating the labours of the months like a larger tapestry showing the hay-month in the Victoria and Albert Museum, London. Formerly in the Collection of Bardac and later of Arnold Seligmann, Paris. Acquired by Sir William in 1934.

German Tapestry
69 David and Bathsheba
Wool and silk, 2ft.10in. × 3ft.2in. (46.27) Probably woven in the Upper Rhineland (Alsace) c.1490–1500 (Kurth, 1, pp.134 and 242) the tapestry shows a messenger acting as go-between King David standing on a drawbridge at the entrance of his palace on the left and Bathsheba seated with her feet in the stream on the right. Her scroll ('Sag · dim · here · was · er · an . mich · begert / des · sol · ersin · gewert') indicates that she is willing to comply with the King's desire. The coats of arms to left and right are those of Heinrich Ingold, merchant of Strassburg, and his wife, Clara Gerbott. A near replica in the Rijksmuseum, Amsterdam, has different inscriptions, no coats of arms, and the costumes have been modernised to conform with early 16th-century fashion. The Burrell tapestry was exhibited at Tours in 1890 (Léon Palustre, *Album de L'Exposition retrospective de Tours*, 1891, p.103). Until 1866 it was in the Collection of Le Carpentier; later in that of Petit de Vauzelles at Saint Symphorien. It was acquired by Sir William in 1935 from E. J. Wythes.

German Tapestry
70 The Pursuit of Fidelity*
Wool, silk, metal, 2ft.6in. × 2ft.10in. (46.28) Probably woven in Upper Rhineland (Alsace) c.1475–1500 (Kurth 1, pp.131 and 238). Fidelity, in the form of a stag, is being chased by a pair of lovers on a dappled-grey horse towards a rope net slung on a hurdle. Above a winding scroll ('ich · jag · nach · truwen · find · ich . die · kein · lieber · zit · gelebt · ich · nie ·) proclaims their mission. A later replica (dated by Kurth to 1500) was formerly in the Engel Gros Collection, Basle. A variant in the Hermitage, Leningrad, in which the lady rides a white horse and the young man stands beside her blowing a horn, bears a different inscription on the scroll: 'Ellend in Freud dich wend ('grief, turn into happiness'). The Burrell piece, formerly in the Kaiser-Freidrich Museum, was later in the Mortimer Schiff Collection, New York. Acquired by Sir William in 1938.

German Tapestry Fragment
71 The Queen of France and the Disloyal Marshal
Wool and linen, 2ft.10in. × 3ft. (46.29) From a long tapestry also probably woven in Alsace c.1475–1500 (Kurth, *Jahrbuch des Kunsthistorischen Sammlungen des Allerhöchsten Kaiserhauses*, Bd.XXXII, 1914, p.13) illustrating the middle high German poem 'Die Königin von Frankreich und der ungetreue Marschall' by the Alemanian poet Schondoch in which the queen as a result of slander is driven into the forest and takes refuge with a charcoal-burner, who in this fragment is directing the king, now aware of the marshal's treachery, and three of his courtiers, towards the pine-wood where the queen is sheltered. The large coat of arms is thought to be that of the Strassburg family of Hochfelden and the tapestry may commemorate the marriage of Agathe von Hochfelden in 1489 with Ludwig Zorn zum Ried, whose arms appear on another portion of the same tapestry. Acquired by Sir William in 1936.

German Tapestry Fragment
72 Two scenes from 'Der Busant'
Wool, silk, and metal, 2ft.6in. × 2ft. (46.31) From a long tapestry probably woven in Alsace c.1475–1500 (Kurth, 1, pp.132 and 240) of which other parts are in the Victoria and Albert Museum, London, and in museums at Cologne and Nuremberg, illustrating a middle-high German poem, based on an earlier French romance, called 'Der Busant' (The Buzzard). On the left of this fragment the English prince and the French princess can be seen resting during their elopement. The prince is contemplating a ring, which he holds between finger and thumb. At this moment in the poem, a buzzard snatches the ring away and the right side shows the prince going in search of it. The two scenes are joined by a twisting scroll with an inscription calling upon God to help him in his search. Failing to find the ring, the prince roams the woods as a wild man. Finally the lovers are re-united and wedded. A replica of this fragment is in the Clemens Collection, Cologne. Acquired by Sir William in 1938.

Swiss Tapestry Strip
73 Four scenes from the Life of the Virgin
Wool and linen, 3ft.2in. × 8ft.6in. (46.46) Probably part of a longer frieze or dorsal, woven in a convent workshop at Basle, c.1475, showing 'The Visitation', 'The Nativity' (combined with 'The Annunciation to the Shepherds'), 'The Adoration of the Kings', and 'The Presentation in the Temple', against a continuous pomegranate-brocaded backcloth. The scenes are depicted side by side without formal division in the centre, where the two figures of St. Joseph, who occurs in both 'The Nativity' and 'The Adoration of the Kings', stand side by side; at either end, however, the inscribed scrolls also partly act as partitions for 'The Visitation' and 'The Presentation'. The little figure of the Dominican nun kneeling beside the crib with a scroll inscribed

'Gloria tibi Domini' may represent the donor, who may also have been the weaver of the tapestry, which is remarkable for its fineness of weave (18 warps to the inch) and its vivid, exceptionally well-preserved, colouring. As in many other tapestries of this date certain features, particularly the whites of the eyes, are accentuated by white linen threads. Formerly in an English private collection; later with A. S. Drey, Munich. (Betty Kurth, 'Vier unbekannte Schweizer Bildwirkereien', *Pantheon*, 6, 1931, p.234). Acquired by Sir William in 1939.

Swiss Tapestry Panel
74 The Wandering Housewife*
Wool, 2ft.7½in. × 3ft.4¾in. (46.39)
This tapestry, possibly a cushion cover, showing a woman riding on a donkey cluttered with various possessions including a baby tucked in a cloth under her chin, besides the spinning staff with which she is busy as she goes along, has been interpreted as a satirical portrayal of the over-active housewife who never gives herself (nor anyone else) a moment's relaxation. Her neurotic expression and the inscription which has been tentatively translated as: 'I have household articles enough, otherwise I would not be so important' seems to support this view of her. Another very similar tapestry from the Clemens Collection in the Kunstgewerbe Museum, Cologne, in which an equally cluttered lady riding a donkey is hailed by a youth, suggests in this example at least that there might be amorous elements involved, for here the lady looks quite young and attractive. Her reply however seems to mean that she is too busy for love. Earlier than these tapestries which were probably woven in or near Basel during the third quarter of the 15th century, is a woodcut of c.1450 entitled the 'wandering juggler' ('Gaukler auf der Wanderung') in the Herzog Anton Ulrich Museum, Brunswick, in which the cluttered lady, spinning as she rides along on a donkey with her possessions which here also

includes a baby suspended in a cradle from her front, a basket of fowls on her head, a neck cloth full of household utensils and various domestic animals, is accompanied by a man, perhaps her husband, who walks beside her. Her expression is intense rather than markedly neurotic but the inscription in which the word 'Sorge' (care) is dominant suggests that here too the satirist's target was the folly of being over-zealous. (Kurth, vol. I, p.99 and p.221).

German or Swiss Tapestry Fragment
75 The Visitation*
Wool, silk, metal, 2ft.5in. × 2ft.5in. (46.45)
Probably woven in north Switzerland or the Upper Rhineland about 1505, doubtless originally forming part of a long narrow tapestry with scenes from the life of the Virgin like the slightly earlier one in the Metropolitan Museum discussed by Vera K. Ostoia (*Bulletin of Metropolitan Museum*, June 1966, p.293) where the same scene occurs in a landscape setting but without the inscribed scroll. The Virgin in both tapestries is characterised by the hook-shaped locks of hair ('Hacken-locken') which Heinrich Göbel (*Wandteppiche*, Part III, I) remarked as typical of a group of tapestries, woven between Basle and Lake Constance in the 15th and 16th centuries, in emulation of south Netherlandish woodcuts. The fragment has been cut to a shield shape to serve as the hood of a cope (in the reproduction in Göbel's first volume on German tapestries, 1933, pl.40, it still retains the fringed border which was added when it was converted for ecclesiastical use). Formerly in the Budge Collection, Hamburg. Acquired by Sir William in 1938.

Swiss or Upper Rhineland Tapestry
76 Hagar and the Angel
Wool, silk, metal, 1ft.11in. × 2ft. (46.40)
This panel and its pair showing 'The Hunt of the Unicorn' were acquired by Sir William in 1937 and were formerly in the Leopold Iklé Collection at St. Gallen (sold 17 September 1923, no.795). At that time

both panels were framed in an elaborate floral border containing the arms of Ludwig Pfyffer of Lucerne who married Frau Salome Bodmer of Baden in 1592 to which year Göbel (part III, 1, p.185, pl.159) ascribes this pair of tapestries, but the border which was removed before its entry into the Collection had as far as is known no original connection with the tapestries which therefore are unlikely to have been woven in connection with this marriage. The panel shown illustrates Genesis, chap.21, v. 14–19.

German Tapestry Cushion Cover
77 Verdure with peacocks
Wool, silk, and metal, 1ft.9in. × 1ft.7in. (47.39)
Probably woven in Lower Saxony during the late 17th century, one of the few tapestries in the Collection later than 1600. Acquired by Sir William by the early years of the century when it can be seen in old photographs as part of the furnishings of his house in Glasgow.

French, Burgundian, Flemish

Franco-Flemish Tapestry
78 Saint Anne, Virgin and Child
Wool, 3ft.1in. × 5ft.11in. (46.14)
The Holy Family is depicted in front of a low wall surmounted by a trellis of flowering plants beyond which is a landscape and strip of sky. On either side of the central group stand St. Catherine on the left and St. Barbara on the right. Tapestry experts have hesitated between the Lower Rhineland and Flanders as the place of origin. Although stylistically related to the latter, long narrow tapestries suitable for use as dorsals and altar-hangings are more characteristic of German production. However, the warps are of wool not linen as in most German tapestries and the narrow shape is probably illusory, the brocaded border top and bottom having been added after the tapestry had been cut. Dr. E. J. Kalf has recently discovered in a private collection

in Holland (ex. Coll. Heilbronner) another tapestry of similar proportions arbitrarily bordered top and sides, with similar brocade-patterned strips depicting 'The Visitation', 'The Nativity' and 'The Flight into Egypt', which was undoubtedly closely associated with the Burrell one. As Dr. Kalf observes the brocade border is reminiscent of the canopy stretched over the Holy Family in the tapestry bearing the armorial shield of Georges de Saluces, Bishop of Lausanne, in the Historisches Museum, Bern, depicting 'The Adoration of the Three Kings', and as the Burrell tapestry is reputed to have come from Switzerland where it hung for some time round the pulpit of a church in the Canton Wallis, there is a good possibility that in their original form the Burrell fragment and its similarly cut companion in Holland would, like the surviving tapestry in Bern, have been about 12ft. in height. The Bern tapestry is thought to have been woven in Tournai about the middle of the 15th century. Formerly in the Henry Howard Collection. Acquired by Sir William in 1937.

French Tapestry Fragment
79 Part of Angel and Landscape
Wool, 3ft. × 2ft.9in. (46.53)
This and another fragment (chiefly depicting a church) in the Collection are believed to derive from the famous Apocalypse of Angers commissioned by Louis I, Duke of Anjou, woven in the workshops of Nicolas Bataille between 1375 and 1379, and given by René of Anjou to the Cathedral of Angers. It was sold in 1843, but subsequently restored to the Cathedral with the exception of certain fragments. Stylised birds in a red ground not unlike those in this fragment are said to occur in two of the Apocalypse scenes, but according to René Planchenault (*L'Apocalypse d'Angers*, 1966, p.31) the Burrell fragments cannot be assigned a definite place in the missing parts of the tapestry. Acquired 1933.

Franco-Flemish Tapestry
80 Arms of Beaufort, Turenne and Comminges*
Wool, 7ft.3in. × 7ft.1in. (46.50)
Part of an armorial tapestry presumably woven for Guillaume III de Beaufort Vicomte de Turenne, who married Aliènor de Comminges in 1349. The four beasts, lion, stag, unicorn and elephant (the latter missing from this fragment) confront one another in diagonal lines wearing mantles on which Beaufort quartering Turenne alternates with Beaufort and Turenne impaling Comminges, each beast being contained within a diamond-shaped enclosure comprising a castle wall with three engaged towers from two of which emerge angels holding a crown over the beast's head. Outside this diamond-shaped motive and as it were reinforcing it are four storks their bodies stretched between rosettes in which Beaufort alternates with Turenne. In 1370 when his brother became Pope Gregory XI, Guillaume III de Beaufort went to live in Avignon and in 1376 when the Pope returned to Rome, he was nominated rector of the Comtat Venaissin. The arms, however, as portrayed in the tapestry, could hardly represent him in this capacity, for as such they would certainly bear the papal insignia as a mark of his delegated authority, but the presence of the storks on the blue ground of the tapestry seems to indicate some association of the Comte de Beaufort with Avignon, for a stork ('cigogne') is the emblem of the 7th-century saint, Agricol, who became the town's patron saint. It seems possible, therefore, that this impressive display of heraldry, one of eight surviving fragments of which two more are in the Burrell Collection, was woven for Guillaume III de Beaufort as Grand-master of some religious-military order connected with the defence of the city. These portions of what was probably a very large tapestry are the only remaining examples of 14th-century heraldic tapestry weaving. Acquired by Sir William in 1929.

Franco-Burgundian Tapestry
81 Peasants hunting Rabbits with Ferrets*
Wool and silk, 10ft. × 9ft.7in. (46.56)
Perhaps a product of Pasquier Grenier's workshop in Tournai, c.1460–70. This fragment, formerly in the Hearst Collection, in which both men and women participate, shows the preparatory stages of the rabbit-hunt – sharpening a staple, taking a ferret from its box, laying nets over the rabbit holes, holding dogs on leash – while a slightly larger portion of what appears to be the same tapestry in the M. H. de Young Museum, San Francisco, shows the trapping and killing of the rabbits. Another hitherto unknown fragment in the Louvre (gift of M. and Mme. Grog-Carven) portraying what may be the same peasants pausing to have a collation, exhibited in the tapestry exhibition at the Grand Palais, Paris, 1973–4 (cat. no.50), would appear to be from a less impressive edition of the same or closely related set. Acquired by Sir William in 1939.

Franco-Burgundian Tapestry
82 Hercules initiating the Olympic Games*
Wool and silk, 10ft.7in. × 12ft.1in. (46.80)
Hercules, dressed in armour and bearing a distinct resemblance to Philip the Good, Duke of Burgundy (1396–1467), is represented in the middle of a throng of contestants which include three Amazonian queens, also identified by inscriptions as Orchias, Ippolite and Menalipe. Above his head another inscription identifies the mountain on which they have congregated as 'Olimppe' and a longer inscription on the scroll above announces in mediaeval Latin: 'Here the warriors with their companions separate with sad heart in order to prepare themselves for the Olympic games now beginning'. The subject was probably suggested by chapter 39 of the *Recueil des Histoires de Troye* by Raoul Lefevre where it is told 'how Hercules began the Olympiades . . . and how he showed his

strength in all manner of games and exercises'. The tapestry however is at variance with this account in that Hercules is represented as a mature man instead of the youth of 15 who initiated the games. The mounted youth beside him who looks nearer the correct age may be intended to represent Philip's son and successor, Charles the Bold, whose first joust at the age of 17 in 1451, the tapestry, possibly woven about 1460–70, may commemorate. Another tapestry, possibly from the same set, is in the Isabella Stewart Gardner Museum, Boston (*Scottish Art Review*, 8, no.3, 1962). Acquired by Sir William in 1937.

Franco-Flemish Tapestry
83 The Pheasant Hunt
Wool and silk, 10ft.7in. × 10ft.11in. (46.61)
In the densely wooded upper half, a royal couple is presented a pheasant by a retainer, while to the left a huntsman aims his crossbow. The lower half in which a male falconer holds a goshawk and a lady falconer bends forward to take a hawk from the lure conforms more closely with the 'mille-fleurs' type of ground. In a publication issued by Messrs. Duveen Brothers in New York, the principal persons are said to be Charles VI of France, Queen Isabel and Odette de Champdivers, but there does not appear to be any genuinely corroborative evidence of this. Stylistically it may be compared with the grape-harvest tapestry in the Cluny Museum, Paris, but the appearance of hennins in a tapestry of the late 15th century is peculiar and may be deliberately anachronistic. Acquired by Sir William in 1936 from the Heilbronner, Duveen and Edson Bradley Collections.

Franco-Flemish Tapestry
84 Rural Dalliance and Fruit-picking
Wool and silk, 9ft.2in. × 14ft.7in. (46.64)
Probably woven in Tournai towards the end of the 15th or beginning of the 16th century, but as Mme Geneviève Souchal points out in her catalogue entry for a related fragment in the Rijksmuseum, Amsterdam (ex. Coll. Schutz) showing a youth in what may be an orange-tree throwing down fruit to a seated lady, when it was shown at the Grand Palais in 1973–4 (cat. no.54), the persons and motives are French rather than Flemish. In this Burrell tapestry the youth is in a pear-tree and the other trees include one bearing pomegranates. Equally fanciful are the two sprites in the foreground mounted on a sheep and a ram tilting at one another with toy windvanes. The tapestry hung in Sir William's dining-room at 8, Great Western Terrace and was lent by him in 1917 to an exhibition of antique furniture and tapestries in Edinburgh (New Gallery, no.24).

Franco-Flemish Tapestry
85 The White Horse
Wool and Silk, 9ft.11in. × 11ft.8in. (46.58)
The huntsman, returning, it seems, from the chase, with a large net folded over the saddle of his white horse, and the hornblower recur among different surroundings in another tapestry (G.-J. Demotte, *La Tapisserie Gothique*, 1924, pl.161). The interest focused on the returning huntsman and his youthful escort by the bag-pipe player, the horn-blower, and woodcutter, suggest that more is involved than is apparent to the eye from this surviving portion. Formerly in the Rita Lydig Collection (sold 4 April 1913). Acquired by Sir William in 1928.

Franco-Flemish Tapestry
86 Alexander and Diogenes
Wool and silk, 10ft.7in. × 12ft.1in. (46.86)
Acquired by Sir William in 1933 as a 'mille fleurs' tapestry representing Charles II of France (1366–1423) going mad in the forest of Le Mans, an incident recorded by Froissart, but probably in fact representing the even more legendary meeting of Alexander and Diogenes, the great philosopher and first of the Cynics, who is said to have lived in a tub and to have told Alexander the Great to stand out of his light. The wooded landscape teems with a mixture of both native and exotic beasts and birds. The tapestry was shown in the retrospective exhibition of Franco-English Art at the Victoria and Albert Museum in 1921 and reproduced in *La Tapisserie Gothique* by G.- J.Demotte (1924, pls.138 and 139).

Franco-Flemish Tapestry
87 An Open-air Meal in the Garden of Love*
Wool and silk, 9ft.7in. × 11ft.10in. (46.66)
Acquired by Sir William in 1945 as 'The Alfresco Banquet', this tapestry in which five persons, attended by a jester and other figures, are seated at table in a landscape, has since been shown to be associated with four tapestries in the Corcoran Gallery of Art, Washington, in one of which the jester and servant pouring soup into a bowl from a ewer recur in reverse. The Corcoran tapestries, hitherto regarded as pleasant scenes of hunting and sheep tending, are now revealed as an allegory of events which culminated on the 22 May 1506 with the signing of the marriage contract between Louis XII's daughter Claude and his cousin and successor, Francis I. In this allegorical context, the open-air banquet becomes a fanciful representation of the nuptial celebrations of Louis XII and his second queen, Anne, Duchess of Brittany, when they met at the Castle of Nantes in January 1499. The Royal couple toast one another across the table while the embracing couple in the foreground is a reminder that their marriage was a matter of love as well as statecraft. Although probably woven in Tournai about 1510, the content is completely French (*Scottish Art Review*, XIV, no.2, 1973, pp.14–21, 38–39).

Franco-Flemish Tapestry
88 Falconers hunting Waterfowl
Wool and silk, 9ft.10in. × 16ft.7in. (46.59)
A party of noblemen and ladies, chiefly mounted on horseback, are hawking in a wooded landscape through which runs a

stream. The unmounted huntsmen carry poles with splayed ends for vaulting over marshy ground. The ease with which both the mounted and unmounted hunters move in relation to their setting anticipates but does not practise a new conception of reality based on perspective. Acquired by Sir William in 1927.

Franco–Flemish Tapestry
89 The Flight of the Heron*
Wool and silk, 10ft.5in. × 10ft.2in. (46.60)
The three huntsmen are bearded, a fashion which did not become established in France until the 1520s, indicating that this tapestry may be considerably later in date than its style might suggest at first sight. It has been suggested that the principal huntsman riding a white horse is a partly fanciful portrait of Francis I showing him at a more advanced age than he could have attained even supposing the tapestry to have been stylistically retarded, as an illustration of Francis I's boast that: 'even when old and ill I shall have myself carried to the hunt'. If so the tapestry may derive from the lost set of 16th-century tapestries depicting the Hunts of Francis I which it has been assumed were used as the prototypes for the surviving 17th-century set made in the workshop of Frans van den Planken and of Marc de Comans in 1618. The latter depict the King at different ages in the various tapestries (*Scottish Art Review*, XIV, no.1, 1973, pp.13–15). Acquired by Sir William in 1936 as late 15th-century 'Combat d'un Héron et un Faucon'.

Franco-Flemish Tapestry
90 Verdure with arms of Miro*
Wool and silk, 11ft.7in. × 10ft.10in. (46.102)
This armorial tapestry, of which there is a drawing by Roger de Gaignières in the Bibliothèque Nationale, shows a development of the 'mille fleurs' ground into more of a landscape setting, perhaps intended to represent a kind of terrestrial paradise teeming with beasts, flowering

plants and fruiting trees, from one of which is suspended a leather shield with the canting arms of Gabriel Miro, doctor in ordinary to the French King, Louis XII (1462–1514). The Ptolomaic sphere between two angels inscribed Ama (love) and Crede (believe) together with the punning motto in the border ('à qui par foy et charité espère · au bo(n) endroit vers lui tourne(n)t le sph(h)ere') proclaim the Lullian belief that a man's fate is not immutably fixed by the constellation in which he is born, as the older astrologers maintained, but that it can be favourably affected by divine intervention if solicited by love and faith. The two flying angels and the armillary sphere recur in a 'mille fleurs' ground beneath a scroll inscribed with the first half of the motto on a tapestry fragment in the Rijksmuseum, Amsterdam. Formerly in the André Jullien de Tonnerre and Brauer Collections. Acquired by Sir William in 1935.

Franco-Flemish Tapestry
91 Mille fleurs with Charity overcoming Envy*
Wool and silk, 8ft.1in. × 7ft. (46.95)
Against a dark blue background covered with clusters of flowering plants, Charity in the guise of a fashionably-attired lady riding astride an elephant, has raised her sword to strike Envy, a cowering knight riding a dog. Above, on a red scroll, are two lines of Latin text: 'Invidi dolor animi cepru peris est proximi · gaudens eius de malis / ut canis · sed hoc elephas nescit vincit et hoc nephas caritas fraceri'. The subject deries from the *Psychomachia* of Prudentius, dating from the 5th-century A.D., of which there were numerous mediaeval transcriptions and adaptations. It probably belonged to a set or formed part of a long tapestry depicting a series of battles between other virtues and vices mounted on allegorical animals woven at the end of the 15th or beginning of the 16th century. Lent to the Glasgow International Exhibition, 1901 (cat. part II,

p.59, no.68) by Sir Thomas Gibson Carmichael, Bart. who sold it at Christie's (2 May 1902, p.38, no.123) either directly or indirectly to Sir William.

Franco-Flemish Tapestry
92 Landscape with Lioness and Doe*
Wool, 8ft.10in. × 11ft.3in. (46.96)
Bought by Sir William in 1929 with the title 'La Force et la Douleur'. A stylised 'mille fleurs' ground is here superimposed on a landscape with three symmetrically arranged clumps of trees in the foreground and the background indicated by a series of boldly receding planes. Perhaps woven in Oudenarde in the early 16th century. Unlike most tapestries of the period it contains no silk and was probably intended to supply the needs of a less exalted market.

Franco-Flemish Tapestry
93 Parc au Cerfs*
Wool and silk, 11ft.8in. × 13ft.10in. (46.133)
One of two very similar tapestries of about 1500 acquired by Sir William in 1933 from Chilham Castle, Kent, differing chiefly in the figures on either side in front of the enclosed park which in this example take the form of a woodman cutting staves on one side and a woman with a bundle of staves burning the end of one of them on the other. In both the deer park is surrounded by an ordinary wattle fence which contrasts strangely with the elaborate gateway with its jewelled spiral columns surmounted by seated lions and its fleurs-de-lis finial, and the studded and strongly bolted oak door guarded on the outside by a fantastic beast chained to a heavy iron ring. The naked sprites playing in the foreground and the pastoral scenes with a bagpipe player among the shepherds and shepherdesses on the far side of the park recur in both tapestries. The sejant lions on the gateway support pennants, checky on the one shown, and paly on the companion tapestry.

Franco-Flemish Tapestries

94   The Camp of the Gipsies*

Wool and silk, 12ft.8in. × 11ft.3in. (46.65)
'While they were thus abusing the belief of many people, their children cut out the purses of those who were attentive to their charms, or they themselves, with the hand with which they seemed to hold an infant (which they did not, for the child was supported by a band put on as a sling, covered over with a blanket, and this hand was free) purloined artfully, without its being perceived.' This description of a visit in 1421 by gipsies to Tournai, in the *Chronique de Flandre*, may have been the original inspiration for the series of tapestries to which this one belongs. 'The History of Carrabarra, so-called of the Egyptians' is known to have been woven in the workshop of Arnold Poissonnier, a fact confirmed on this tapestry by the top border of hanging bells. In front, on the right, a young buck is having his purse purloined by one charmer while his fortune is told by another. In the midst of the music-making and dalliance, the gipsy mothers wash and nurse their babies. The rectangular insertions upper left and right seems to be taken from another tapestry in the same set or even a missing part of the same tapestry. The one on the left showing dead sheep suspended by their legs from the side of a camel recurs in a tapestry of about 1500 called 'The Egyptians' in the Cranbrook Academy of Art, Michigan, U.S.A. Acquired by Sir William in 1935.

Franco-Flemish Tapestry

95   The Camel Caravan*

Wool and silk, 11ft.9in. × 21ft.3in. (46.94)
One of a group of about 15 tapestries associated with the workshops of Jean and Antoine Grenier (sons of Pasquier) and of Arnould Poissonnier and variously described in their accounts as 'à la manière de Portugal et de l'Indie, l'histoire de Calcou' and other titles. A procession of exotic beasts organised by the Portuguese at Antwerp in 1502 is said to have aroused great popular interest. The Indians, as distinct from the Portuguese, are dressed in blankets and chiefly engaged in peddling. A tapestry showing the Giraffe caravan from a related set is in the Victoria and Albert Museum, London. Acquired by Sir William in 1937.

Franco-Flemish Tapestry

96   Verdure with thistles*

Wool, 8ft.8in. × 8ft.1in. (46.108)
Unlike the 'mille fleurs' tapestries in which the flowering plants are scattered on a coloured background as in a wallpaper design which theoretically can be extended in any direction indefinitely, this portion of a verdure with thistles can only be extended at the sides, as each plant extends upward the whole height of the tapestry which is terminated at the top by stylised clouds. Another portion, seemingly from the same tapestry as the Burrell one, is in a museum in Copenhagen, and a fragment of a related tapestry without the stylised clouds is in a French private collection. According to Betty Kurth (*Kunstmuseets Aarskrift*, 1940, p.56) these thistle hangings may be from the set ordered by Peter II, Duke of Bourbon (d.1503) in memory of his ancestor Louis II. The white thistle heads surrounded by blue rings are said to allude to 'La ceinture d'espérance' in the devise and coat of arms of Louis II. Doubtless there were also sets ordered by others. In 1518, for example, Peter van Aelst sold 341 aunes of green tapestry decorated with thistles to Charles V. Acquired 1936.

Franco-Flemish Tapestry

97   God appearing to Moses

Wool and silk, 10ft10in. × 13ft. (46.137)
One of a set (originally two sets) of Sibyl tapestries of about 1500–10 from Rothamsted, of which three more complete ones and two fragmentary ones are in the Collection. The Sibyls, the oracles of pagan antiquity, were introduced into Christian iconography to supplement the role of the prophets whose function of foretelling the birth of Christ they also assumed. In this tapestry God the Father is seen appearing to Moses on Mount Horeb. The other tapestries show pairs of Sibyls standing in a similar verdure composed of branching stems with large serrated leaves and fantastically shaped blooms on either side of an ornate fountain. Moses is here shown removing his shoes 'for the place whereon thou standest is holy ground' (Exodus, chap. 3, v. 5).

Flemish Tapestry Fragment

98   Beatrix Soetkens in Bed*

Wool and silk, 5ft.4in. × 4ft.1in. (46.126)
From the first scene in the first tapestry of a set of four depicting the 'Legend of Our Lady of Sablon' commissioned by François de Tassis, Master of the Imperial Posts, and possibly designed by Bernard van Orley. The legend concerns the appearance of the Virgin Mary to a pious seamstress called Beatrix Soetkens at Antwerp to instruct her to remove from its resting place in the local church a little statue known as 'Our Lady of the Branch' ('Onze Lieve Vrouw op Stocxken') and take it to the Church of the Sablon in Brussels. The fourth tapestry is in the Brussels Museum and is dated 1518, and another tapestry from the set is in the Hermitage, Leningrad. The two remaining tapestries were cut by Frederick Spitzer in order to accommodate them in the armour gallery of his mansion in Paris. Subsequently the vertical fragment was cut horizontally, removing the standing figure of the Virgin and Child at whom the old seamstress is gazing in wonderment (M. Crick Kuntziger, *La Tenture de la Légende de Notre Dame du Sablon*, 1942, pp.12–16, pl. v). Acquired 1938.

Anglo-Netherlandish

Anglo-Netherlandish Tapestry

99   Verdure with the arms of Robert Dudley, Earl of Leicester

Wool and silk, 9ft.7in. × 8ft.2in. (47.1)
One of a pair from Drayton House, Northamptonshire, acquired by Sir William in 1932 originally designed to flank

a larger hanging with the same arms surmounted by the bear and ragged staff, which were introduced into the arms of Leicester in 1561, when his elder brother Ambrose was made Earl of Warwick. It has been suggested they may have been made in connection with the Earl's visit to Warwick in 1571 when the chancel of St. Nicholas was hung with arras and tapestry or with that of Queen Elizabeth to Kenilworth in 1575, or with Leicester's visit in 1585 as High Commissioner to Holland, where it is today usually assumed they were woven, although the Earl is known from a record dated 27 November 1571 in the Black Book of Warwick to have encouraged a local tapestry weaving industry, similar to the one established by Sheldon of Beoley. Acquired 1932.

Anglo-Netherlandish Tapestry
100   The Luttrell Table Carpet
Wool, silk, metal, 6ft.4in. × 18ft.1in. (47.3)
The central field of the table carpet, an interlocking complex of squares, circles and quatrefoils enclosing daisies, roses and honeysuckle, bears three coats of arms, and the running plant patterned border twelve coats of arms of differing shape at irregular intervals. The central shield with the arms of Luttrell impaling Wyndham above the initials AL stands for Sir Andrew Luttrell of Dunster whose marriage with Margaret, daughter of Sir Thomas Wyndham of Felbrigg in Norfolk, took place in 1514 when they were both minors. Sir Andrew died in 1538, being survived by his widow for more than 40 years. In her will, dated 9 March 1580 she bequeathed 'my best and longest carpett' to her daughter, Margaret Edgecumbe, from whom it descended to Lord Mount Edgecumbe of Cotehele House, Cornwall. It may have been commissioned by Margaret Luttrell in memory of her husband and their marriage just as the Lewknor table carpet (dated 1564) the only other surviving 16th-century tapestry woven table carpet (now in the Metropolitan Museum, New York) was apparently commissioned 21 years

after the death of Sir Roger Lewknor by his widow. The designer might conceivably have been the Flemish painter, Hans Eworth, who was active in England from about 1545 to 1573 and acquired a reputation as designer of costumes and décor as well as portraiture. He painted portraits of Lady Margaret's son and of her half-brother and as an immigrant would presumably have been well-qualified to arrange for the weaving of the table carpet in the Netherlands. Acquired by Sir William in 1928.

Stained Glass

Heraldic Terms:
Impaled is the division of a shield into two equal parts by a vertical line.
Quartered is the division of a shield into quarters or any number of parts formed by vertical and horizontal lines.
Dexter is the actual right-hand side, i.e. to the observer's left, of the shield.
Sinister is the actual left-hand side, i.e. to the observer's right, of the shield.
The catalogue numbering of coats of arms on quartered shields is horizontally from left to right, dexter preceding sinister.

Armorial Glass from Fawsley Hall – 16th century

In 1950 Sir William acquired a series of 39 shields from the banqueting hall at Fawsley Hall, near Daventry in Northamptonshire, the residence of the ancient family of Knightley from 1416 until the death of Rainald, Baron Knightley of Fawsley in 1895. In so far as the stained glass is concerned the key-figure in this pedigree is Sir Edmund Knightley, who is believed to have rebuilt the house at Fawsley between 1537 and 1542 (the year of his death) and to have embellished it with the armorial glass now in the Burrell Collection. His marriage with Ursula, sister and co-heiress of John Vere, Earl of Oxford, accounts for the presence in the house of the seven contemporary roundels commemorating the ancestry of his wife. His own ancestry is recorded in the more or less rectangular panels with hour-glass shaped shields. Also in the house were four ornate medallions perhaps added by Sir Richard Knightley, who died in 1615 aged eighty-two, and who perhaps also added the three garter medallions, one of which is certainly for William Parr, Earl of Essex, brother of Katherine Parr. (A more detailed description with reproductions of this series is given in the *Catalogue of Stained and Painted Heraldic Glass in the Burrell Collection*, 1962, nos.115–53.)

Seven roundels with shields of the de Vere family

101 John de Vere (1442–1513), 13th Earl of Oxford, P.C., K.G. (Dexter: (1) and (4) De Vere; (2) and (3) Howard; Sinister: (1) and (4) Montagu quartering Monthermer; (2) and (3) Neville). Dia. 16¼in. (45.325)
Second, but first surviving son of John de Vere, 12th Earl, and Elizabeth Howard; married Margaret, daughter of Richard Neville, Earl of Salisbury by Alice, daughter of Thomas Montagu, 4th Earl of Salisbury; Hereditary Lord Great Chamberlain of England.

102 Robert de Vere (b.1257), 6th Earl of Oxford (De Vere impaling Mortimer). Dia. 16in. (45.326)
Robert, 6th Earl, married Margaret, sister of Edmund, 1st Lord Mortimer, of Wigmore, and daughter of Roger de Mortimer.

103 Hugh de Vere (c.1210–c.1263), 4th Earl of Oxford (De Vere impaling De Quincy). Dia. 17¾in. (45.330)
Hugh, 4th Earl, married Hawise, daughter of Saher de Quincy, 1st Earl of Winchester; officiated as Master Chamberlain of England at the coronation of Queen Eleanor in 1236.

104 Richard de Vere (b. c.1385), 11th Earl of Oxford, K.G. (De Vere impaling Sergeaux quartering Arundel). Dia. 16in. (45.328)
Richard, 11th Earl, married Alice, sister and co-heir of Richard Sergeaux, and third daughter of Sir Richard Sergeaux by Philippe, daughter and co-heir of Sir Edmund of Arundel; fought at Agincourt; K.G. May, 1416.

105 De Vere impaling Hume (vert a lion rampant argent langued or). Dia. 17¾in. (45.331)

106 De Vere impaling Clare (or three chevrons gules). Dia. 17in. (45.329)

107 De Vere impaling Marshal, Earl of Pembroke (per pale or and vert a lion rampant gules). Dia. 18¼in. (45.327)

108 Large shield-shaped panel with the helm, mantling (ermine), crest (a buck's head coupled argent attired or), supporters (golden falcon for Skenard and blue boar for de Vere) and shaped shield of Sir Edmund Knightley of Fawsley (d.1542) and his wife Ursula Vere; (Dexter: (1) and (17) Knightley; (2) and (18) Duston; (3) and (13) Skenard; (4) and (14) Harowdon; (5) and (15) St. John; (6) and (16) Bagot; (7) and (23) Burgh; (8) and (24) Cowley; (9) and (19) Combemartin; (10) and (20) Lion; (11) and (21) Dillon Lee; (12) and (22) Thorleys; Sinister: De Vere quartering Howard.) 30¾ × 18½in. (45.332)
'Sir Edmund Knightley . . . added a splendid shield to the Knightley matches for his wife was a sister and co-heir of John Vere, the 14th Earl of Oxford. He is said to have finished the work upon the great hall at Fawsley where his arms are in the window supported by the blue boar of Vere and the golden falcon of the Skenards . . . He left no one of his six daughters surviving at his death and Fawsley was in turn enjoyed by Sir Valentine Knightley.' (*Northamptonshire Families*, ed. Barron, 1906, p.171.) For the arms of Sir Valentine, brother of Sir Edmund, see cat. no.134.

Six hour-glass shaped shields with the arms of Sir Edmund's paternal ancestors

109 John Knightley of Gnosall, Staffordshire, and his wife Elisabeth Burgh (Dexter: (1) and (4) Knightley; (2) and (3) Duston; Sinister: (1) and (4) Burgh; (2) and (3) Cowley). 19½ × 16½in. (45.295)
John Knightley of Gnosall (d.1413), 8th in the line of descent, married Elisabeth, daughter of Adam Burgh, and grand-daughter and heir of William of Burgh of

Burgh Hall in Gnosall, which William had married Eleanor, daughter and heir of John Cowley of Cowley. By this marriage Burgh Hall came to the Knightleys.

110 Knightley (quarterly ermine and paly of six gules and or) quartering Duston (azure a buck's head cabossed or) and Burgh (argent on a saltire sable five ducks of the field). 19½ × 17in. (45.296)
The fourth quarter is a replacement.

111 Richard Knightley of Gnosall and his wife Joan Giffard (Knightley impaling Giffard). 19½ × 16½in. (45.298)
Joan Giffard, wife of Richard Knightley of Gnosall, 9th in line of descent, was probably daughter of John Giffard of Chillington in Staffordshire.

112 Giffard (azure three stirrups or with their leathers) impaling Cowley (gules a chevron compony or and argent between three crosses flory of the last). 19¾ × 16¾in. (45.305)

113 Richard Knightley of Fawsley and his wife Elizabeth Purefoy (Dexter: (1) Knightley; (2) Duston; (3) Burgh; (4) Cowley; Sinister: (1) and (4) Purefoy, co. Bucks.; (2) and (3) Purefoy, co. Leicester). 19½ × 16½in. (45.294)
Richard Knightley (d.1443), 10th in line of descent, was the first Knightley of Fawsley, co. Northampton, which manor he acquired in 1416. His wife was the daughter of Thomas Purefoy of Drayton.

114 Purefoy, co. Bucks. (gules three pairs of hands couped hand in hand) quartering Purefoy, co. Leicester (azure three stirrups or) impaling Duston (azure a buck's head cabossed or) quartering Foulshurst (gules fretty or a chief argent) and Catesby (argent two lions passant sable crowned or). 19½ × 17in. (45.304)
Richard Knightley held the manor of Fawsley jointly with his wife Elizabeth and Robert Catesby.

Fourteen hour-glass shaped shields with the arms of Sir Edmund's maternal ancestors

115 Dillon-Lee (argent a fess azure between three crescents gules) impaling Thorleys (gules on a chief argent five lozenges gules fesswise). 19½ × 16½in. (45.299)

116 Dillon-Lee quartering Thorleys. 19 × 16in. (45.300)

117 St. John (gules two bars argent, a canton ermine) impaling Bagot (argent a chevron gules between three martlets sable). 19 × 16½in. (45.301)

118 St. John (gules two bars argent a canton ermine) quartering Bagot (argent a chevron gules between three martlets sable). 19 × 16in. (45.303)

119 St. John (gules two bars argent a canton ermine) quartering Bagot (argent a chevron gules between three martlets sable) impaling Combemartin (gules a lion rampant vair). 19¼ × 16¼in. (45.302)

120 St. John (gules two bars argent a canton ermine) quartering Bagot (argent a chevron gules between three martlets sable) Combemartin (gules a lion rampant vair) 19½ × 16½in. (45.297)

121 Harowdon (argent on a bend gules five lozenges or) impaling St. John, Bagot, Combemartin, Lion, Dillon-Lee and Thorleys. 18 × 15¾in. (45.309)

122 Harowdon quartering St. John, Bagot, Combemartin, Lion, Dillon-Lee and Thorleys; 17¾ × 16in. (45.310)

123 Harowdon quartering St. John, Bagot, Combemartin, Lion, Dillon-Lee and Thorleys impaling Vaux (chequy argent and gules on a chevron azure three cinquefoils or) quartering Sharpe (argent three rooks' heads erased sable). 17¾ × 15½in. (45.313)

124 St. John, Bagot, Combemartin quartering Lion, Dillon-Lee, Thorleys. 17 × 14¾in. (45.315)

125 Lion (argent a lion rampant gules) impaling Dillon-Lee (argent a fess azure between three crescents gules) quartering Thorleys (gules on a chief argent five lozenges gules fesswise). 18 × 15½in. (45.314)

126 Lion quartering Dillon-Lee and Thorleys. 17¼ × 16in. (45.311).

127 Skenard (sable a chevron between three hawks' lures argent) impaling Harowdon, St. John, Bagot, Combemartin, Lion, Dillon-Lee, Thorleys. 17¼ × 15¼in. (45.317)
This shield is for Henry Skenard and his wife Margery, sister and heir of Thomas Harwedon (or Harowdon). Their daughter Jane married Sir Richard Knightley (d.1534), 12th in the line of descent, and the shields of their sons, daughter, and grandson are shown in cat. nos.108, 134, 135, and 136. Jane Skenard, wife of Sir Richard, died about 1539 and was buried with her husband in Fawsley Church where their tomb remains.

128 Skenard quartering Harowdon, St. John, Bagot, Combemartin, Lion, Dillon-Lees, Thorleys. 18 × 15¾in. (45.312) The shield for Sir Richard Knightley and his wife Jane Skenard, i.e. Knightley impaling Skenard, is missing from the series.

Four hour-glass shaped shields with the royal arms and the cross of St. George

They may have been added in honour of Sir Edmund's father who had been made a Knight of the Bath.

129 King Edward The Confessor (azure a cross patonce between five martlets or in orle). 18 × 16in. (45.306)
Arms attributed to various early kings and adopted by Richard II and University College, Oxford.

130 Royal Arms of England (France and England quarterly). 18 × 16in. (45.307) The side segments bear the red roses of Lancaster (with abraded yellow centres).

131 Castile (gules a castle or) and Leon (argent a lion rampant gules) quartering Aragon (paly of eight or and gules) and Sicily (per saltire argent two eagles displayed sable and paly of eight gules and or). 17¾ × 15¾in. (45.308) The side segments bear the split pomegranates of Aragon. These two shields were doubtless for Henry VIII and his first wife Catherine of Aragon (marriage annulled in 1533).

132 St. George (argent a cross gules). 17¾ × 15½in. (45.316) This shield in combination with the royal arms may be for Henry VIII as Sovereign of the Order of the Garter.

Four shaped medallions perhaps added by Sir Edmund's nephew, Sir Richard Knightley (d.1615)

133 Henry VIII and Jane Seymour (France and England quarterly impaling (1) Seymour augmentation; (2) Seymour; (3) Beauchamp; (4) Esturmy; (5) MacWilliam; (6) Coker. Inscribed 'Dieu et Mon Droyt, 1580'; 24 × 16½in. (45.318)

134 Sir Valentine Knightley (d.1566) and his wife Anne Ferrers (Dexter: (1) Knightley; (2) Duston; (3) Burgh; (4) Cowley; (5) Skenard; (6) Harowdon; (7) St. John; (8) Bagot; (9) Lion; (10) Combemartin; (11) Dillon-Lee (12) Thorleys; Sinister: (1) Ferrers of Groby; (2) Ferrers; (3) Botetourt; (4) or a cross gules; (5) Mountford; at fess point a crescent argent. Inscribed: 'Sir Valentine Knightley Fares 1572'. 24 × 18½in. (45.319) Sir Valentine was the third son of Sir Richard Knightley by Joan Skenard to own Fawsley Hall, and he became the ancestor of all succeeding Knightleys, the six daughters of his elder brother Sir Edmund having died young. He married Anne

Ferrers, daughter of Sir Edward Ferrers of Baddesley Clinton in Warwickshire. She died in 1554.

135 Sir William Spencer (d.1532) of Althorp, and his wife Susan Knightley (Dexter: azure a fess ermine between three seamews' heads erased argent for Spencer; Sinister: Knightley quarterly of twelve) Inscribed 'Sir William Spencer Knightley, 1572.' 23¾ × 17½in. (45.320)
Susan Knightley, sister of Sir Valentine, married Sir William Spencer of Althorp, from whom descended the Dukes of Marlborough and the Earls Spencer. Her eldest brother, Richard Knightley of Upton (d.1537), married her husband's sister, Jane Spencer.

136 Sir Richard Knightley (d.1615) and his wife Mary Fermor (Dexter: Knightley quarterly of twelve as in cat. nos.134 and 135; Sinister: argent on a fess sable three anchors or between three lions' heads erased gules). 23½ × 18¼in. (45.321)
Sir Richard, eldest son of Sir Valentine Knightley, died in 1615 at the age of eighty-two. His first wife, Mary Fermor died in 1573 and he married secondly Elizabeth Seymour, daughter of the Duke of Somerset.

Three garter medallions perhaps added by Sir Richard Knightley (d.1615)

137 Ambrose Dudley, Earl of Warwick, K.G. (1) Somery; (2) Beaumont; (3) Grey; (4) Belesme, for Talbot; (5) Beauchamp; (6) Newburgh, for Warwick; (7) Guildford; (8) Mortimer; at fess point a besant. 26½ × 17in. (45.324)

138 William Parr, Earl of Essex, K.G. (1) Parr; (2) Parr; (3) Fitzhugh; (4) Garnegan; (5) Furneaulx; (6) Grey; (7) Marmion; (8) Garnegan; (9) St. Quintin; (10) Green; (11) Mablethorpe). 26¾ × 17½in. (45.323)
William Parr (1513–1571), brother of Katherine Parr, sixth and last queen consort

of Henry VIII, was the son and heir of Sir Thomas Parr, of Kendal, Westmorland, and of Parr in Prescot, Lancashire, by Maud, daughter and co-heir of Sir Thomas Green, of Green's Norton, Northants. He was made Earl of Essex and Knight of the Garter in 1643; Marquess of Northampton 1546/7; attainted 1553 with loss of earldom and other honours; restored as marquess 1558/9.

139 Royal Arms of England (France and England quarterly). 26¼ × 14¼in. (45.322)

14th, 15th, and 16th century Armorial Glass of Various Families

Cat. nos.140–243 comprise a selection of the 48 panels of glass illustrated and described in the *Catalogue of Stained and Painted Heraldic Glass in the Burrell Collection*, 1962, which also included some donor panels of heraldic interest.

140 Beatrix van Valkenburg (d.1277); daughter of Dirk II, Lord of Valkenburg (Limburg) and third wife of Richard, Earl of Cornwall, King of the Romans. She is kneeling and wears a mantle (barry gules and sable). In the blue surround are a number of roundels charged with an Imperial Eagle, three of the upper roundels being partly obliterated by a white letter inscription: 'Beatrix de Valkenburch Regina Allemannie'. 24 × 10½in. Oxford School, late 13th century. Probably from the Church of the Minorites, Oxford, where she was buried. Ex-Coll: George William Jerningham, 8th Baron Stafford of Costessey. Lit: C. Woodforde, *English Stained and Painted Glass*, 1954, p.6. (45.2)
It is not certain that the red and black bars on the mantle should be interpreted as a blazon. They are not the arms of either her father or her husband, and may be a replacement.

141 Lisle (or on a chief azure three lions rampant of the first) impaling Stourton (sable a bend or between six fountains). Dia.13½in. 15th century. (45.135)

142 Roundel with unnamed shield (azure a saltire or), perhaps for St. Alban's Abbey or town. Dia.8in. 15th century. (45.69)

143 Garland, co. Lincs. (gules two bars or in chief three besants). 12½ × 10½in. 15th century. (45.170)

144 Kneeling lady donor and shield of Chalons, co. Devon (gules two bars ermine between nine martlets argent). 17½ × 23⅞in. 15th century. (45.39)
The panel appears to be composed of heterogeneous elements.

145 Shield set in an ornamental canopied surround with two eagles and two lions (Howard quartering Plantagenet and Delapole). 24¾ × 22in. Norwich School c.1475. Ex. Coll: George William Jerningham, 8th Baron Stafford of Costessey. (45.131)
These are the arms of John Howard (1430–1485) 1st Duke of Norfolk the Yorkist leader, who was killed at Bosworth field in 1485 fighting for Richard III. He was descended by his mother, a Mowbray, from Thomas de Brotherton, Earl of Norfolk, second son of Edward I—hence the lions of England in the second and third quarters.

146 Royal Tudor Arms (France and England quarterly), perhaps for Henry VII. 12 × 10½in. Late 15th century. (45.188)
The forepart of the bottom leopard in second quarter is restored with lion of later date.

147 Beauchamp (gules, a fess between six martlets or) as borne by various branches of the Beauchamp family. Dia. 11in. 15th century. (45.130)

148 Shield set in an ornamental surround similar to cat. no.145 (De Vere quartering Howard and Chaucer). 24 × 22in. Norwich School, c.1475. Ex Coll: George William Jerningham, 8th Baron Stafford of Costessey. (45.132)
John de Vere (1442–1513), 13th Earl of Oxford, the Lancastrian leader at the

Battle of Bosworth, was son of Elizabeth, daughter and heiress of Sir John Howard, grandfather of Sir John Howard, 1st Duke of Norfolk (see cat. no.145). They were therefore first cousins He died at Hedingham Castle, for which it is supposed these two panels were made

149 Roger de Mortimer, 4th Earl of March and Ulster (d.1397) (Mortimer quartering De Burgh). 10½ × 8½in. 14th century. (45.115)

150 Shield (azure two swords in saltire points downwards) suspended by a strap from a tree, perhaps for Sir John Scrymgeour, Constable of Dundee (d. c.1460–61); 13½ × 8in. 15th century. (45.175)

151 Champney (argent, three bars nebuly gules) impaling Lecheche (chequy or and azure two bars gules). 10¾ × 9½in. 14th century. (45.114)

152 Shield (gules, two lions passant guardant or) perhaps for King John before his accession to the throne in 1199. 9 × 7in. 13th–14th century. Lit: Newton, *Scottish Art Review*, vol. VIII, no.4, 1962. (45.122)
The same arms were used by King John's nephew, Henry, Count Palatine of the Rhine, and his heirs, and an illegitimate son, Richard de Varenne.

153 Shield (or, two lions passant in pale azure) of Sir John de Somery, of Dudley Castle, Worcs. 20½ × 17½in. Early 14th century. Ex Coll: Bruce, sold Christie's 28.6.1935. Lit: Newton, *Scottish Art Review*, vol. VIII, no.4, 1962. (45.109)
The barony of Dudley was held by the family of Somery from 1194 until 1322 when Sir John de Somery died.

154 Clare, Earls of Hertford and Gloucester (or three chevrons). 8½ × 6¾in. 14th century. (45.121)

155 Neville (gules a saltire argent) impaling Audley (gules fretty or). 10½ × 9½in. 14th century. (45.287)
Ralph, 2nd Lord Neville married Alice, daughter of Hugh de Audley in 1326/7.

156 Shield (gules, three lions passant guardant or, a label of three points azure) perhaps for Edward II before his accession. Dia. 11in. York School, 14th century. Ex Coll: Dr. Philip Nelson. (45.129)

157 Nettervill (or a cross gules fretty argent). 9½ × 7¾in. 14th century. (45.116)

158 Chedworth (azure a chevron or between three wolf's heads erased of the last) impaling Gray (vert a lion rampant within a bordure engrailed argent). 8¼ × 7½in. 15th century. (45.168)

159 Sir John de Haudlo (argent a lion rampant azure guttee d'or crowned or). 17 × 18¼in. 14th century. (45.111)

160 Shield (azure a cross patonce between five martlets or) perhaps for King Edward the Confessor. 9 × 7in. 15th century. (45.176)

161 Fitzhugh (azure, three chevrons braced, a chief or). 8½ × 7¾in. 14th century. Ex Coll: Sir Hercules Read (sold Sotheby's 9.11.1928, lot 716 as 'from Tanfield Church, Yorks.'). Exhib: B.F.A.C (British Heraldic Art). 1916, p.118, no.2. (45.124)
The chief is a modern replacement.

162 Roundel with badge or crest (an eagle displayed or). Dia. 6½in. 14th century. Ex Coll: Dr. Philip Nelson. (45.128)
Eagle badge of Edward III.

163 Blundevill (quarterly per fess indented or and azure, a bend gules); 8¾ × 7½in. 14th century. (45.123)

164 Neville (azure a lion rampant or). 9 × 7¼in. 15th century. (45.126)

165 Bereford (or three fleurs de lys sable) in a barbed quatrefoil. 16¾ × 18¾in. 14th century. (45.112)

166 Sir John de Ryvers (or masculy gules). 11¼ × 8¼in. Early 15th century. Ex Coll: Dr. Philip Nelson. (45.173)

167 Sulliard, co. Essex (argent a chevron gules between three pheons sable). 8¾ × 7¼in. 15th century. (45.145)

168 Ford, Abbey Field, co. Chester (per fess or and ermine a lion rampant azure fretty argent and gules). 18 × 9½in. 16th century. (45.199)

169 Davies, co. Sussex (argent a chevron sable between three spur revels gules) impaling Moreton (ermine a chief dancetty gules). 8⅜ × 7¼in. 15th century. (45.146)

170 Bazley (azure three fleurs de lys argent). 8½ × 7in. 14th century. (45.117)

171 Glastenbury, co. Dorset (or a bend fusilly sable). 15 × 15in. 14th century. (45.113)

172 Massey (gules three fleurs de lys argent). 8½ × 7in. 14th century. (45.118)

173 Stringer, Whiston Sharleston, co. York (sable, three eagles displayed erminois). 8¼ × 7½in. 16th century. (45.217)

174 Griffith Hampton quartering Haynes impaling Cave. 28 × 12in. 16th century. (45.200)
Anne Cave, wife of Griffith Hampton was the daughter of Antony Cave of Chicheley, co. Bucks, by Elizabeth, daughter of Thomas Lovet of Astwell.

175 Unnamed shield (or an eagle displayed azure over all on a fess wavy argent three mullets sable). 8½ × 7½in. Probably Flemish, 16th century. (45.218)

176 Challers, co. Cambridge (argent a fess between three annulets gules) quartering Servington (ermine a chevron azure). 10¾ × 10in. 15th century. (45.155)

177 Herys (per fess gules and vert three hedgehogs proper). Dia. 12½in. (mounted). 16th century. Ex Coll: F. S. Eden; Hearst (New York). (45.236)

178 Beaumont, Bretton, co. York (gules a lion rampant within an orle of crescents argent). 11 × 9in. 15th century. (45.157)

179 Sir Roger Wentworth of Codham Hall, Essex (d.1539) and his wife Anne Tyrrell (d.1534); (Dexter: (1) and (4) Wentworth; (2) and (3) Howard; (5) Despencer; (6) Goushill; (7) Tibetot; (8) Badlesmere. Sinister: (1) Tyrrell; (2) Hellyon; (3) Rolfe; (4) Swynbourne; (5) Botetourt; (6) Gernon 14 × 12in. 16th century. (45.197)

180 Red rose of Lancaster encircled by fragmentary garter motto. Dia. 15in. 16th century. (45.191)

181 Sir John Wentworth of Gosfield Hall, Essex (d.1567) and his wife Anne Bettenham (d.1575); (Dexter; (1) and (10) Wentworth; (2) and (11) Despencer; (3) and (12) Howard; (4) and (7) Hellyon; (5) and (8) Swynbourne; (6) and (9) Botetourt; Sinister: Bettenham). 14 × 12in. 16th century. (45.198)
Sir John, eldest son of Sir Roger (see cat. no.179) was knighted in 1547. He and his wife, Anne, were buried in the Wentworth Chapel in Gosfield Church where their tomb bears an armorial shield of Wentworth, quarterly of fourteen, impaling Bettenham.

182 Paynell (or two bars azure an orle of martlets sable within a bordure argent). 10¾ × 10in. 16th century. (45.215)

183 Heath (argent, three ogresses, the first charged with a cross crosslet argent) impaling Kerville (gules a chevron or between three leopards' faces argent). 7½ × 6½in. 15th century. (45.150)

184 Neville of Hornby (argent a saltire gules a label of three points argent). 11 × 9in. 15th century. (45.156)

185 Angel holding the shield of Tierney (argent a chevron sable a chief gules) impaling Wydville (argent a fess and quarter gules) quartering Woodhouse (gules a cross or between twelve crosses crosslet fitchee argent) and Redeswell (argent a chevron gules fretty or between three hinds' heads in profile gules); fragmentary architectural canopy with crocketted pinnacles in blue field. 40 × 16in. 15th century. (45.134)

186 Upsale (argent a cross sable) within a fragmentary border. Dia. 15in. 15th century. (45.138)

187 Huddesfield (argent on a fess between three boars passant sable a crescent argent) impaling Matford, co. Devon (argent a chevron gules between three quatrefoils slipped vert). 8¾ × 7½in. 15th century. (45.153)

188 Philpot (sable a bend ermine) impaling Chideok (gules an escutcheon between eight martlets in orle argent) within a fragmentary border. Dia. 16in. 15th century. (45.136)

189 Holland (per pale indented or and gules) quartering Lucy (azure three lions rampant argent) and Dreux (ermine) and impaling Chideok (gules an escutcheon between eight martlets in orle argent) within a fragmentary border. Dia. 16in. 15th century. (45.137)

190 Erpingham (vert an escutcheon between eight martlets in orle argent) impaling Clopton (sable a bend argent between two cotises dancetty or). 9¼ × 8¼in. 15th century. (45.154)

191 Fitzalan of Arundel (gules a lion rampant or) quartering Maltravers (sable fretty or) within a fragmentary border. Dia. 15in. 15th century. (45.192)

192 Angel holding a shield bearing the Royal Arms of England prior to 1340 differenced by a label of three points argent; seemingly a companion panel to cat. no.185 but with a differently shaped architectural canopy. 39¾ × 16in. 15th century. (45.38a)

193 Arma Christi (the Sacred Heart and four wounds in a blue field). 12½ × 11in. 15th century. Ex Coll: A. L. Radford (said to be from the Becket window in Canterbury Cathedral). (45.378)

194 Arma Christi (gules a cross crowned with thorns vert between in chief four nails and in base two scourges, over all a reed with sponge in bend dexter and a spear in bend sinister). 9¼ × 8in. 15th century. (45.12)

195 Battle Abbey (argent a cross gules charged at fess point with a bishop's mitre argent and or, between in the first and fourth quarters a sword erect gules pommelled or and in the second and third quarters a crown or). 13 × 10½in. 14th century. Lit: Eden, *The Connoisseur*, September 1930, p.174, and January, 1931, p.43; Newton, *Scottish Art Review*, vol. VIII, no.4, 1962. (45.120)
The Benedictine Abbey of St. Martin at Battle was founded by William the Conqueror and dedicated in 1095 by Anselm, Archbishop of Canterbury.

196 Henry Spencer, Bishop of Norwich (1370–1406) (Despencer within a bordure charged with eight mitres or). 8 × 7in. 15th century. (45.151)
The warlike Bishop of Norwich who suppressed Litester's rebels in 1381.

197 Grocer's Company (argent a chevron gules between nine cloves sable, three, three, and three) within a floral border. Dia. 13in. 16th century. (45.240)
The Worshipful Company of Grocers (anciently called the Pepperers) was incorporated 16 February, 1428, and received a grant of arms in 1531

198 Unnamed shield of a bishop (sable the hand of St. Thomas vested or touching the Sacred Heart gules between three spear heads or impaling argent a mitre ensigned with an archiepiscopal cross in bend sinister or). 8 × 7½in. 15th century. (45.152)

199 Merchant Adventurers (barry nebuly or and azure on a chief gules a lion of England quartering azure two roses or (sic for gules)). 17½ × 23in. Norwich School, 15th century. (45.40)
The Society of Merchant Adventurers (or

Hambrough Merchants) was incorporated in 1296. The chief is quartered in reverse of the normal order.

200 Canterbury, Priory of Christ Church (azure a cross argent charged with the letter X) impaling Gryndal (quarterly or and azure a cross quarterly ermines and or between four peahens collared counterchanged). $8\frac{1}{2} \times 7\frac{1}{2}$in. 16th century. (45.208)
Edmund Gryndall, Archbishop of Canterbury, 1576–1583, received a grant of arms in 1559.

201 Philippe de Villiers de L'Isle Adam, Knight of Malta ((1) and (4) de Villiers de l'Isle Adam; (2) and (3) de Chastillon; over all on a chief gules a cross throughout argent for the Sovereign Military Order of Malta). $7\frac{1}{4} \times 6\frac{1}{2}$in. 16th century. Ex Coll: Lord Rochdale. (45.291)
Later 13th Grand Master of the Sovereign Military Order of Malta (from 1530 until his death in 1534). See G. R. Gayre, *The Heraldry of the Knights of St. John*, 1958.

202 Canterbury, Priory of Christ Church, impaling Edmund Gryndal, Archbishop of Canterbury, 1576–1583. Identical with cat. no.200. (45.209)

203 Chertsey Abbey (per pale azure and or two keys in bend sinister and a sword in bend dexter points upward). $8\frac{1}{4} \times 7\frac{1}{4}$in. 15th century. (45.125)
The Benedictine Abbey at Chertsey, Surrey, was founded by Earconwald, Bishop of London, during the 8th century A.D.

204 Magdalen College, Oxford (lozengy ermine and sable in a chief of the second three lilies argent) within motto 'Sanct Nomen eius fecit michi magna qui potens est'; Dia. $20\frac{1}{8}$in. Late 15th century. (45.139)
The College of St. Mary Magdalen was founded by William Waynflete, Bishop of Winchester (licence granted 1457), whose arms became those of the College.

205 Abbey of Bury St. Edmunds (azure three crowns or). $9 \times 6\frac{3}{4}$in. 15th century. (45.119)
The crown in base is not original.

206 See of Winchester (gules two keys addorsed or in bend sinister interlaced with a sword argent in bend dexter). $11\frac{1}{2} \times 9\frac{1}{2}$in. 15th century. (45.143)

207 Trinity College, Cambridge (argent a chevron between three roses gules seeded or, in chief gules a lion of England between two closed books or). $9\frac{3}{4} \times 7\frac{1}{2}$in. 16th century. Ex Coll: Lord Rochdale. Lit: Eden, *The Connoisseur*, XCIV, 1934, p.81, repro. VII. (45.361)
The arms of Trinity College, founded in 1546, were confirmed at the Visitation of 1575.

208 Unnamed shield ((1) and (4) azure on a fess sable a portcullis between two fleurs de lys or; (2) and (3) gules an eagle displayed or; on an inescutcheon sable two keys in saltire and a crescent or). $9\frac{1}{2} \times 7\frac{3}{4}$in. 16th century. (45.336)

209 Brent, co. Kent (gules on a wyvern's tail nowed argent a mullet sable). $9\frac{1}{8} \times 7\frac{7}{8}$in. 15th century. Ex Coll: Dr. Philip Nelson. (45.171)

210 John Copleston, of Copleston, co. Devon (argent a chevron engrailed gules between three leopards' faces azure langued gules). $8\frac{1}{4} \times 7\frac{3}{4}$in. 15th century. Ex Coll: A. L. Radford (in library of Bovey House). Lit: M. Drake, *History of English Glass Painting*, 1912, pl.XII, fig.6 (as from St. Edmund's-on-the-Bridge, Exeter). (45.147)
Drake notes remarkable use of double insertion, the tongues of the leopards being inserted into the faces which are themselves inserted into the field.

211 Brent (gules on a wyvern's tail nowed argent a mullet sable) impaling Bosville (argent on a chevron azure three mullets or). $9\frac{1}{8} \times 7\frac{3}{4}$in. 15th century. Ex Coll: Dr. Philip Nelson. (45.172)

212 Unnamed shield (or a chevron ermine fimbriated gules between in chief two crosses flory and in base a horse's head erased sable). $8\frac{7}{8} \times 7\frac{1}{8}$in. 15th/16th century. (45.335)

213 Fitzalan (gules a lion rampant or) quartering Warenne (chequy or and azure). $11\frac{1}{4} \times 9\frac{1}{4}$in. 14th century. (45.127)
Perhaps for Richard Fitzalan, 4th Earl of Arundel (beheaded 1397).

214 Bery (or three bars and in chief a crescent gules) impaling Chichester, co. Devon (chequy or and gules, a chief vair). $8\frac{1}{2} \times 7$in. 15th century. (45.165)

215 Cope (argent on a chevron azure three lilies or all between three roses gules seeded or leafed and slipped vert) impaling Cruwys (azure a bend per pale indented argent and gules all between six escallops or). $10 \times 9\frac{1}{2}$in. 16th century. Ex Coll: Lord Rochdale. Lit: Eden, *The Connoisseur* XCIV, 1934, p.81, repro. VI. (45.292)
Sir Anthony Cope married Jane Cruwys. He was Chamberlain to Katherine Parr and died in 1550.

216 Cruwys, of Cruwys Morchard, co. Devon (azure a bend per pale indented argent and gules all between six escallops or). 9×7in. Ex. Coll: A. L. Radford (in library of Bovey House). 15th century. (45.140)
Said to be for Thomas Cruwys (living 1460) son of John Cruwys. The ruby glass in the bend is modern.

217 Cope impaling Cruwys. Identical with cat. no.215 (45.239)

218 Winterbourne (argent a fess sable goutty of the first between three water-bougets of the second) in fragmentary yellow stained surround. Dia. $12\frac{1}{2}$in. 16th century. (45.160)

219 Lewknor (argent three chevrons azure) impaled by Lovelace (gules on a chief indented sable three martlets argent) quartering Lovelas (azure on a saltire engrailed argent five martlets sable) within a wreath caught by gadrooned golden clasps. Dia. 13in. Inscribed 'John Lewknor, 1548'. Ex Coll: Hearst, New York. (45.237)

220 Radford (quarterly of four) impaling St. Ermine (quartering Morton and Lovain). Dia. 10¾in. 16th century. Ex Coll: Lord Rochdale. Lit: Eden, *The Connoisseur* XCIV, 1934, p.81. (45.293)
The second and fourth dexter quarterings may be for Felbich and Aske.

221 Withypoule (per pale or and gules three lions passant guardant in pale within a bordure all counterchanged) quartering Pembrigg and Forester within a fragmentary yellow stained border. Dia. 14½in. 16th century. (45.225)

222 Comberworth (chequy or and gules on chief argent a lion passant sable) impaling Kardeleke (azure a tower embattled or). Dia. 12¼in. 15th century. Ex Coll: Lord Rochdale. Lit: Eden, *The Connoisseur*, XCIV, 1934, p.5, repro. IV. (45.178)

223 Comberworth impaling Allanson (azure three fleurs de lys or within a bordure gules). Dia. 12¼in. 15th century. Ex Coll: Lord Rochdale. Lit: Eden, *The Connoisseur*, XCIV, 1934, p.5, repro. V. (45.179)

224 Jernegan or Jerningham (argent three buckles lozengy gules) impaling Harward (azure on a fess paly of six gules and vert between three owls argent a mullet of the last). Dia. 12in. 15th century. Ex Coll: Oswald Barron. Exhib: College of Arms, London (Herald's Commemorative Exhibition), 1934, no.154. (45.174)
An ancestor of the barons Stafford of Costessey Hall, some of whose collection of stained glass is in the Burrell Collection. (See cat. nos.140, 145, and 148).

Cat. nos.225–43 include 16th century badges, rebuses and monograms

225 Oval medallion with badge of Henry VIII (a portcullis or) ensigned by a royal crown and enclosed by a wreath of oak leaves and red roses. 17½ × 12½in. 16th century. Ex Coll: Hearst, New York. (45.234)
A gold portcullis was used by both Henry VII and Henry VIII as a badge with the motto 'altera securitas' (possibly deriving from a pun on the name Tudor, i.e. two-door but Fox-Davies (*Heraldic Badges*, 1907, p.53) notes that it was also used by the Beauforts who had no Tudor descent).

226 Four quarries: (1) the initial W. and the monogram P. L. joined by a loveknot issuing from a flower and heart and terminating in two sea-shells. 6½ × 5¼in. 16th century. (45.107); (2) and (3) badge of Courtenay, co. Devon (a dolphin embowed). 6¼ × 4⅝in. 16th century. (45.163 and 164). (4) Fetterlock badge. 5¾ × 4½in. 16th century. Ex Coll: Sir Hercules Read. Exhibited: B.F.A.C. 'British Heraldic Art', 1916, p.119, no.9. (45.213)
A Fetterlock badge is attributed to Arthur, Prince of Wales (son of Henry VII); Richard Plantagenet (d.1460), Duke of York; and Henry Bourchier (d.1483), Earl of Essex.

227 Oval medallion with badge of Henry VIII and Jane Seymour (a fleur de lys on two wings conjoined in lure or) ensigned by a crown and within a border similar to cat. no.225. 17½ × 11¾in. 16th century. Ex Coll: Hearst, New York. (45.235)

228 Roundel with the Rose of York (sable a rose argent seeded or) within a black border studded with yellow; Dia. 6¼in. 16th century. Ex Coll: A. L. Radford (Bovey House). (45.162)
On the rose is scratched: 'Peter Cole glazier made all ye heads of these windows 1765'. It was on loan to the Victoria and Albert Museum, London, in 1915.

229 Large quarry comprising four smaller quarries: (1) crowned initial R. perhaps for Richard III; (2) a white hart lodged perhaps for Richard II; (3) the white lion of March for the Duke of York; (4) the plantagenista and initials h.B. perhaps for Harry Brome (Bolingbroke). 11 × 9in. 16th century. Ex Coll: Sir Henry Ellis; Sir Hercules Read, (sold Sotheby's, 9.11.28, lots 714–5). Exhibited: B.F.A.C. 'British Heraldic Art', 1916, p.120, no.11, pl.XXVI (quarry with the white lion of March). (45.219)
According to Sotheby's sale catalogue these quarries formed part of a collection made by Sir Henry Ellis to illustrate a series of letters read at the Society of Antiquaries in 1822 on royal badges (see also cat. nos.231 and 233), but there is no trace of any such letters in *Archaeologia*.

230 Roundel with the monogram L.T. within a spiral leaf border. 7⅜in. 16th century. Ex Coll: Eumorfopoulos. (45.70)

231 Large quarry comprising four small quarries: (1) crowned initial R. perhaps for Richard III; (2) and (3) crowned fleur-de-lys between the initials E. and R. perhaps for Edward VI; (4) the plantagenista between the initials h.B. perhaps for Harry Brome (Bolingbroke). 12½ × 10in. 16th century. Ex Coll: Sir Henry Ellis; Sir Hercules Read, (45.220). (See also cat. nos.229 and 233)

232 Roundel with the Sacred Monogram I H C crowned. Dia. 7¾in. 16th century. Ex Coll: Eumorfopoulos. (45.80)

233 Large quarry comprising four small quarries: (1) the Bosworth thornbush enfiling a royal crown with the initials H. and E. perhaps for Henry VII and Elizabeth of York; (2) and (3) the plantagenista (broom-plant) perhaps for Harry Brome (Bolingbroke); (4) a crowned rose of York. 12 × 9¼in. 16th century. Ex Coll: Sir Henry Ellis; Sir Hercules Read, Exhibited: B.F.A.C. 'British Heraldic Art', 1916, p.119, no.4. (45.221) (See also cat. nos.229 and 231)

234 Roundel with the monogram H. R. or H. B. within a spiral leaf border similar to cat. no.230. Dia. 7¾in. 16th century. Ex Coll: Eumorfopoulos. (45.81)

235 Panel with roundel containing the monogram W. B. $12\frac{3}{4} \times 12\frac{3}{8}$in. 16th century. Ex Coll: Sir Hercules Read. (45.211)
Sold with cat. no.237 as lot 710 at Sotheby's 9.11.28; the initials are for William Bradbridge, Bishop of Exeter, 1571–8.

236 Large quarry comprising four small quarries each with the rayed monogram J.S. $12 \times 9\frac{1}{4}$in. 16th century. (45.158).

237 Panel with roundel containing the shield of the Diocese of Exeter (argent two keys addorsed in saltire, in pale a sword up-pointed) and on either side the initial R. and the monogram I. S. $12\frac{3}{4} \times 12\frac{1}{4}$in. 16th century. Ex Coll: Sir Hercules Read, (45.212). (See cat. no.235)

238 Roundel with the Eagle, symbol of St. John the Evangelist, perched on the Book of Revelation, with inscribed scroll: 'In principio erat verbum et verbu erat'. Dia. $8\frac{1}{8}$in. 15th century. (45.61)

239 Large quarry with the rebus of John Islip (d.1532), Abbot of Westminster (a man slipping from a tree clutching a severed branch, i.e. slip, between the representation of an eye and the word 'SLIP'). $12 \times 9\frac{1}{2}$in. 16th century. Lit: Tanner, *Scottish Art Review*, 1962, vol. VIII, no.4. (45.223)
Perhaps painted for the Chantry Chapel of Abbot Islip in Westminster Abbey, or some other part of the abbey 'in the windows whereof (saith Camden) he had a quadruple device for his single name; for somewhere he set up an eye with a slip of a tree; in other places an I with the said slip; and in some places one slipping from the tree with the word Islip' (J. Weever, *Ancient Funerall Monuments*, 1631, p.488). A carved stone head, believed to represent John Islip, the last of the great abbots of Westminster, is preserved in the abbey (Lit: Tanner, *Westminster Abbey Quarterly*, 1939, vol. I, no.1). Some other examples of the Islip rebus in stained glass are discussed by F. Sydney Eden, *The Connoisseur*, April 1924, p.204.

240 Roundel with the Eagle, symbol of St. John the Evangelist, perched on a mound with an inscribed scroll issuing from its beak: 'In deo te confido'. Dia. $8\frac{1}{8}$in. (45.62)

241 Panel comprising thirteen quarries, some identified as badges, (1), (2), and (3) three plant sprigs including the Rose and Columbine for Henry IV; (4) and (5) portcullis for Henry VII and VIII; (6), (7) and (8) two plants and the burial of Reynard the Fox; (9) a white falcon gorged with a ducal coronet for Richard II; (10) and (11) the rose-en-soleil for Edward IV; (12) a flower with eight petals; (13) ears of barley, said to be for Wydville. $22\frac{1}{8} \times 16\frac{3}{4}$in. 16th century (45.102)

242 Panel with thistle, perhaps for Scotland (but not crowned). $5\frac{3}{4} \times 5$in. 16th century. (45.228)

243 Panel comprising thirteen quarries, some identified as badges and crests, (1) a griffin's head erased; (2) a running man-headed tiger; (3) an eagle's head guttee de larmes erased holding a flower sprig in its beak, said to be for Walcot; (4) a stork; (5) a panther passant, perhaps for Henry VI; (6) a rebus of William Middleton, a bird prched on a barrel with inscribed scroll: 'W. Middil-t-un' and the black letter 't' between; a stag statant surrounded by the letters 'A. I. B. C. ff. p.' said to be the rebus of Buckland; (8) similar to (6) above; (9) and (10) two birds; (11) the initials 'h' and 'p' joined by a chain; (12) a bird and merchant's mark; (13) a demi-bull, rampant or, said to be for Bulmer. $22\frac{1}{8} \times 16\frac{1}{2}$in. 16th century. (45.102)

12th to 17th century Figured and Ornamental Stained Glass

Cat. nos. 244–82 are some of the smaller examples of French, German, English, Flemish, Swiss, and Dutch stained glass of the 12th to 17th century illustrated and described in the *Catalogue of Stained and Painted Glass in the Burrell Collection*, 1965.

244 Tracery figure of a Censing Angel, nimbed, kneeling to right, holding censer in right and censer boat in left hand. 7×8in. English, 14th century. Ex. Coll. Eumorfopoulos. (45.32)

245 Rectangular panel with the full-length figure of the Prophet Jeremiah holding a scroll inscribed: 'novu(m) faciet (dominus) sup(er) t(e)r(r)a(m) femina circu(m)dabit virum'; he stands or possibly sits with the scroll unfolded in front of him between the slender columns of an arcade. 24×13in. French, mid-12th century. Lit. Wentzel, *Pantheon*, September–October, 1961, pp.247–9. fig.11. Perhaps identical with the 'stained glass panel representing a Saint (sic) holding a banderole bearing an inscription' acquired by Sir William Burrell from Arnold Seligmann on 23 April, 1923. (45.364)
Probably derives in a somewhat restored condition from the windows of St. Denis which were despoiled during the French Revolution and subsequently replaced in a much restored state by Viollet-le-Duc. The remaining fragments are among the earliest examples of French stained glass and of special interest in that they were probably inspired by Abbot Suger, who reformed and rebuilt the Abbey and who wrote a famous description of the windows. Other portions of the window have been shown by M. Grodecki to be in the Church of Twycross, Leicestershire, to which they were given by Sir John Waltham Waller about 1840.

246 Tracery roundel of abstract design in yellow, blue and black. Dia $6\frac{7}{8}$in. English, 14th century. (45.20)

247 Medallion with the Sacrifice of Isaac depicted in a red ground enclosed by a black and white barbed sexfoil border edged with blue; Abraham (thus inscribed top centre in white letters reserved in black) holds Issac facing him in a crouching position on the sacrificial altar. Dia. $18\frac{1}{2}$in. Germany (middle or upper Rhine), mid-13th century. Lit. Wentzel, *Pantheon*,

May–June, 1961, p.108, fig.1. (45.488) Removed from the Church of St. Thomas at Strassburg in 1775. Seven other medallions are in the Strassburg Museum and one in the Museum at Stuttgart.

248 Rectangular panel with the figure of the Virgin Mary interceding for three resurrecting souls represented by the busts of a woman in green, a man in yellow and boy in blue, their hands raised in prayer. $30\frac{1}{2} \times 8\frac{1}{4}$in. Swiss (Constance), c.1310. Ex Coll. Hearst. Lit. R. Becksmann, *Die Architektonische Rahmung des Hoch-Gotischen Bildfensters*, 1967, S. 31 und S. 81, Abb. 61 und 62. Exhib. McLellan Galleries, Glasgow, 1951, no.491. (45.480)
From the same window as cat no.249 and together forming the two flanking lights of a three light window respresenting a Deesis, the missing central light being occupied by the figure of Christ as judge. Their small size suggests a village church or the chapel of a larger one.

249 Rectangular panel with the figure of St. John the Baptist interceding for three resurrecting souls represented by the busts of a man in yellow, a girl in pink, and a boy in blue. $30\frac{1}{2} \times 8\frac{1}{4}$in., Swiss (Constance), c.1310–20. Ex Coll. Hearst. Lit. Wentzel, *Pantheon*, May–June 1961, p.108, figs.4 and 6. Exhib. McLellan Galleries, Glasgow 1951, no.491. (45.480)

250 Shaped window head with blue gable top surmounted by yellow leaf finial; diapered green ground of differing pattern; running vine border in white and yellow reserved in black with fragments of red ground. $7\frac{3}{4} \times 9$in. English, 14th century. (45.18)

251 Lancet-shaped panel with the figure of a bearded male Saint standing under an ogival arch with slender columns. $24\frac{1}{2} \times 9\frac{1}{2}$in. English (Norwich School), 14th century. Ex. Coll. Barons Stafford of Costessey Hall, Norfolk; F. W. Bruce. Exhib. McLellan Galleries, Glasgow, 1951, no.494. (45.24)

A standing female saint (described as St. Mary Magdalene) also from the Costessey Collection is in the Victoria and Albert Museum, London, and another panel from the same window is in St. Louis, U.S.A. (See also cat. no.253).

252 Roundel having grotesque reserved in ringed black ground on patchily red-tinctured glass; human upper half of figure wears jesters hood and cape and looks downward, wielding a club; lower part of the body is that of a furry creature of bear or cat family, speckled black, with bushy flame-like tail; presumably later white border inscribed: 'Domini 1577'. Dia. $8\frac{1}{2}$in. English, 14th century. (45.17)
Grotesques of this kind are a characteristic feature of 14th century East Anglian manuscript illumination such as the *Luttrell Psalter* (c.1340).

253 Lancet-shaped panel with the figure of St. John, apostle, standing under an arch with slender columns; he gazes three-quarter right holding the poisoned cup with winged serpent in his right and a a palm in his left hand; scroll inscribed: 'pass su noster ico natus eo maria virgine'; $25 \times 11\frac{1}{2}$in. English (Norwich School), 14th century. Ex Coll: Barons Stafford of Costessey Hall, Norfolk; F. W. Bruce, Exhib: McLellan Galleries, Glasgow, 1951, no.504. (45.25)
Of a slightly larger size than cat.no.251 and without the ogival arch and the red and gold stars in the diapered blue ground, but presumably from the same church.

254 Roundel with two monks, half-length in front of a shrine; one holding a staff and a rosary; the other a large book with a yellow clasp; he bows his head in sorrow or penitence and his taller companion regards him sadly or possibly reproachfully. Dia. 13in. English 14th century. Ex Coll. Lord Rochdale. Lit. Eden, *The Connoisseur*, xciv, 1934, p.5, (45.35)
Possibly related to a fragmentary mid-15th century panel in the Bodleian Library,

Oxford, showing the Penance of Henry II before the Shrine of Thomas à Becket.

255 Rectangular tracery panel with kneeling angel holding a chain (? of censer) in a niche with cusped ogival arch; two pairs of wings; emerging from rayed blue clouds; red ground with two sunbursts upper band with lozenge flanked by sunbursts. $20\frac{1}{2} \times 11\frac{1}{2}$in. English (Norwich School) 15th century. (45.56)

256 Rectangular panel showing King David and a messenger, the young king enthroned on the left, while a messenger hands him, or is handed by him, a letter; the king wears an ermine-lined mantle and the messenger, bearded, in armour, wears a green surcoat with yellow lettered hem ('A pace domin . . . noster'); a young man and an elderly man with a woman slyly peeping over his shoulder stand in attendance; the entrance to the chamber is filled with warriors and beyond is a cavalcade of mounted soldiers; patterned tiled floor with white dog in foreground. 27×19in. Flemish, 16th century. Ex Coll. Marquess of Abergavenny, Eridge Castle, Kent. Exhib. McLellan Galleries, Glasgow, 1951, no.329. (45.414)
Possibly from the same cycle as the panel from the Neave Collection in the Prittlewell Parish Church, Southend-on-Sea, showing the Death of Saul and the Coronation of David.

257 Roundel with man warming himself at fireside representing February from a set of the Months; seated in an oak arm-chair; he has removed one soft buckskin slipper and is holding his foot and hands towards the open grate in which a cauldron bubbles over leaping flames; a towel hangs on a rail projecting from the stone wall which is pierced by a window slit; black and white tiled floor. Dia. $9\frac{1}{2}$in. English (Norwich School), 15th century. Ex Coll. Dr. Philip Nelson. (45.83)
Said to be from the same set as three roundels of the later 15th century in the Victoria and Albert Museum (September,

October and November) which are thought to have been originally in St. Michael-at-Coslany Church, Norwich, later in the parsonage and then in a school which replaced it (see Woodforde, *The Norwich School of Glass Painting in the 15th century*, 1950, p.153). February is represented by a man warming himself at the fireside with one shoe removed in the Bedford Book of Hours (Brit. Mus. Add. 18850, f.2) made in France, c.1420. The Burrell roundel is probably at least fifty years later. A close parallel in English illumination is to be found in a Book of Hours which belonged to Henry VII of c.1485 (Brit. Mus. Add. 17012, f.2) where the man is seated on a stool warming hands and foot.

258 Rectangular panel with angel and scroll in a quatrefoil; the angel emerging from rayed blue clouds with outstretched hands wearing amice and alb; the scroll inscribed: 'Te eternu(m) patre(m) omnis t(er)ra veneratur'; red ground inside the quatrefoil and blue with a rayed star or sunburst of different shape in each corner. 16 × 25in. English (Norwich School), 15th century. Ex Coll. Lord Rochdale. Exhib. McLellan Galleries, Glasgow, 1951, no.333. Lit: Eden, *The Connoisseur*, XCIV, 1934 (July), p.5. (45.94)
The inscription is from the Te Deum Laudamus, v.2 ('All the earth doth worship thee, the Father everlasting').

259 Narrow rectangular panel showing the 'Presentation in the Temple', with the Virgin Mary kneeling facing left in the foreground while Simeon, vested in red with blue and yellow stole standing on the far side of the altar, receives the Child; a man and two women are seen beyond in the vaulted ambulatory of a gothic church with five traceried windows in grey and yellow stain. 49¼ × 23¼in. German (Rhineland), late 15th century. Ex Coll Barons Stafford of Costessey; Bruce. Exhib. McLellan Galleries, Glasgow, 1951, no.466. Lit. M. Drake, *The Costessey Collection of Stained Glass*, 1920, no.64. (45.513)

Described by Professor Alfred Stange as a very fine example of the work of the Meister der Heilige Sippe (Cologne). It probably derives, therefore, from one of the secularised Rhineland churches.

260 Rectangular panel showing the 'Miracle at Cana' with the marriage feast taking place in a timber barrel-vaulted room; the guests, which include Christ, the Virgin Mary and two disciples, and the crowned bride between two women, are seated at two tables, one projecting as an arm from the other; as a servant pours the new wine into a tumbler, Christ, in profile facing right, leans forward intently; and two minstrels blow a fanfare. 40¾ × 22¼in. German (Rhineland), late 15th century. Ex Coll. Barons Stafford of Costessey. Lit. M. Drake, *The Costessey Collection of Stained Glass*, 1920, no.18; W. Wells, *Scottish Art Review*, vol. VI, no.4, 1958, p.8 (repro). (45.426)
Probably from the Rhineland and from the same set of windows as a panel of identical size showing the 'Presentation in the Temple' now in the north wall of the nave of Thursley Parish Church, Surrey (Costessey cat. no.15, plate XIII).

261 Roundel showing man and woman at table representing the month of January from a series of the Months, in brown enamel and yellow stain; the interior of room with a man and woman seated in a box settle on the far side of a trestle table set with food and drink; the woman, who wears a dress, raises her glass to the man in fur hat and fur-lined overcoat slit at the sides; inscribed at the top: 'Januar'. Dia. 8½in. Flemish, late 15th century. (45.428)
Six panels from an earlier and slightly smaller series from Cassiobury Park, now in the Victoria and Albert Museum, possibly of English origin, and other similar representations of the Months are described by Herbert Read, *Burlington Magazine*, vol. XLIV, 1923, p.167). (See also cat. no. 263).

262 Rectangular panel showing a peasant in brown enamel and yellow stain on white; standing, spade in hand, wearing a stiff round wide-brimmed hat; shoulder length hair; girdled tunic and kilt; leggings and soft laced leather shoes; at his hip a pouch and long knife; landscape setting with trees on the left and on the right a farm house and horses harrowing a field. 9 × 6¾in. Flemish, 16th century. (45.466)

263 Roundel showing a man and woman at fireside representing the month of February from a series of the Months in brown enamel and yellow stain on white; the man wearing a fur hat and fur-collared gown over an undergarment which covers his head, holds out his hands, to a log fire blazing in the hearth while his wife, kneeling fans the fire with bellows; inscribed upper centre: 'Fevrier'. Dia. 8½in. Flemish, late 15th century. (45.429)
See also cat. no.261.

264 Rectangular panel showing men and women round a column in delicate shades of pink, blue, green and yellow; on a fluted column in the centre stands the effigy of a warrior (Mars) in full armour holding lance and shield; round it are four men, one bearded, and four women garlanded with leaves and holding hands; on the right a young man plays a pipe and drum; landscape setting with fortress upper left and trees on right. 27 × 18½in. French, 16th century. Ex Coll. Dr. Martin Erdmann. Exhib: McLellan Galleries, Glasgow, 1951, no.520. (45.77)

265 Roundel with the figure of St. Catherine of Alexandria standing in a landscape depicted in brown enamel and yellow stain; facing, nimbed and crowned, holding sword, point downward, above the hub of her wheel; on her other side is the vanquished pagan emperor; rocks to left and castle to right. Dia. 9in. Flemish, early 16th century. (45.440)

266 Roundel depicting the 'Annunciation' in brown enamel and yellow stain; the Virgin, facing, seated in swooning posture to the right beneath the Dove, with the Angel descending from the left; architectural setting with tiled floor and column in front of a round arched, vaulted porch and glimpse of fortress beyond. Dia. 9in. Flemish, early 16th century. (45.442)

267 Small rectangular monolith panel with the figure of St. Servatius in the vestments of a bishop holding crozier and key standing in an arched surround of black, with reserved sprays of foliage delicately nuanced with yellow stain; the arch itself, outlined in white with trefoils in the spandrels, is without shafting on the right side. $5\frac{1}{4} \times 3\frac{5}{8}$in. German (Lower Rhineland). c.1330–40. Lit. Wentzel, *Pantheon*, May–June, 1961, p.108, fig.8 (45.475)
St. Servace, Bishop in Tongern and Maastricht, was especially venerated in the Lower Rhineland.

268 Small rectangular monolith panel with the figure of St. John the Baptist holding the Agnus Dei standing in an arched surround of black with reserved sprays of ivy in white and yellow stain; $5\frac{1}{4} \times 3\frac{5}{8}$in. German (Lower Rhineland), c.1330–40. Lit. Wentzel, *Pantheon*, May–June, 1961, p.108, fig.7. (45.476)
See cat. no.267.

269 Small shaped panel with grape picker cutting a bunch of grapes to put in a basket at his feet; facing left, wearing skull cap with chin strap, girdled tunic with sickle at his hip, leggings and shoes. $5\frac{3}{4} \times 2\frac{3}{4}$in. French, 15th century. (45.401)

270 Small rectangular panel comprising three fragments joined together; (1) top left: a scaly monster in black and yellow stain on white beneath a band of dotted roundels; (2) bottom left: a somewhat similar winged dragon swallowing a male or female figure (St. Margaret of Antioch?) in a black ground diapered with plants; (3) right: a shepherd, seen from the back, holding crook, wearing hooded and belted garment, and ankle pads, in black ground

with white and yellow plants. $7 \times 9\frac{1}{4}$in. English, 15th century. (45.63)

271 Roundel with kneeling figure of a youth snaring birds in a meadow, a bird cage with bird in it beside him; behind him a part of a wall or building and a wattle fence; the youth dressed in hat with upturned brim, girdled garment and soft shoes. Dia. $6\frac{1}{4}$in. English (Norwich School), 15th century. Ex Coll. Dr. Philip Nelson. Lit. C. Woodforde, *The Norwich School of Glass Painting in the 15th century*, 1950, p.154. (45.76)
According to Woodforde this roundel, acquired by Dr. Nelson in Norwich, probably formed part of a series of Months and represented September or November.

272 Rectangular panel with winged putto and grotesque in a part violet and part green ground; the putto in grisaille with blue wings and yellow hair, kneeling, facing right, holding a yellow lance whose tip he thrusts into the gaping mouth of a yellow monster with scrolling body. $10\frac{3}{4} \times 13\frac{1}{2}$in. French, early 16th century. (45.405)

273 Rectangular panel with putto and grotesque similar to cat. no.272 but facing to the left. $10\frac{3}{4} \times 13\frac{1}{2}$in. French, early 16th century. (45.406)

274 Shaped panel with bust of the Virgin Mary; downcast head and sorrowing expression; white head-cloth with yellow border; blue dress. $11\frac{3}{4} \times 12$in. French, 16th century. Ex Coll. Eumorfopoulos. (45.416)

275 Roundel with the 'Temptation' in brown enamel and yellow stain; Adam on the left leans against a tree with two apples in his outsretched hand; Eve, standing against a tree on the right, one hand resting on a branch, and the human-headed serpent coiled above her head; yellow landscape with buildings. Dia. 9in. Flemish 16th century. (45.444)

The figures are taken from an engraving by Marc Antonio Raimondi (after a drawing by Raphael). A maiolica panel with similar figures in the Victoria and Albert Museum, London, is dated 1523.

276 Rectangular panel depicting an allegorical subject with man surrounded by vices and virtues; in the centre a bearded, half-naked man walks clasping his hands in contrition ('Homo'); he gazes earnestly at another bearded naked man holding a chopper in one hand and a birch in the other ('Conscientia') and he is followed by a young woman with clasped hands and bowed head ('Tristitia'); facing man from the other side are an elderly fully draped woman ('Avaritia'), a young woman with wild expression and hand raised to her head ('Opinio'), and a woman biting a heart ('Invidia'); a large matron, wearing a peacock-plumed helmet, with puffed chest and arms akimbo, follows on the right ('Superbia'). 8×9in. Flemish, 16th century. (45.464)

277 Small square panel depicting a scene of pageantry and mock tournament taking place in a courtyard in black and brown enamel and yellow stain on white; on the right the marshall or constable on horseback with three other officials on foot also clad in black, their backs to an oak door, watch a column of soldiers, sword in hand, with a halberdier in charge of them, swagger through the yard while three trumpeters on the left blow a fanfare; in the centre a combat involving three figures, possibly mummers, takes place and at the rear in a gap between the castle walls two boys armed with wooden swords standing on platforms held by soldiers make passes at one another. $6\frac{1}{2} \times 6\frac{1}{2}$in. Swiss, 16th century. (45.499)

278 Oval medallion showing a horseman and woman; the man, wearing black hat and white ruff, stick in left hand, on horse plunging to right; the woman standing in black dress with white cap, ruff and apron, holding tumbler and

ewer; between them a tree. 9½ × 7¾in.
Dutch, 17th century.
(45.568)

279 Oval medallion with Roemt Roomen
in his workshop seated at a bench making
roofing tiles; turned to right in black hat,
white collar, brown coat, apron,
knee-length breeches and blue stockings,
with various tools on bench, wall and
paved floor; in the wall facing him shelves
stacked with tiles and in the windows to
the rear two white and yellow stained
glass medallions; below is an inscription
containing the tilemaker's name, the
words: 'Het decken is myn ampt' (tiling
is my trade') and the date 1660. 9½ × 7¾in.
Dutch, 17th century. (45.554)

280 Small octagonal panel showing
Harmen Lohman at work in a kitchen;
the cook, ruddy in the glow of a roaring
fire, stirs the contents of a cauldron, while a
boy seated beside him turns the spit on
which two small carcases are roasting; on
the right is a built-in dresser; below is an
inscription with the name 'harmen Lohman'
in bold lettering followed by four lines of
cursive writing, mostly erased, ending
'1686'. 8¼ × 5½in. Dutch, 17th century.
(45.551)

281, 282 Two rectangular panels with part
of a repeating pattern of intersecting circles
traced in yellow enclosing quatrefoils in
alternating areas of blue and red; narrow
border of white glass down one side.
35½ × 22½in. German (Erfurt), early 14th
century. Lit. Wentzel, *Pantheon*, May–June
1961, p.106, fig.2. Exhib. McLellan
Galleries, Glasgow, 1951, no.458. (45.482)
From the Augustinerkirche in Erfurt,
where there still remains in one of the
three windows of the choir two consecutive
bands of similar patterned glass (reproduced
by Heinrich Deutsch, *Glasmalereien des
frühen 14 Jahrhunderts in ost-mittel
Deutschland*, 1958, pp.125 ff., pl.14, fig.28).
The windows appear to date from the
early 14th century when the choir of the
church was built (between 1298 and 1313?)

Three-Light Window from the Carmelite Church, Boppard-on-Rhine

In addition to the smaller panels of stained
and painted glass, the Burrell Collection
contains some larger windows or parts of
windows, among which is the important
series from the Carmelite Church,
Boppard-on-Rhine, which includes three
separate lancet windows as well as the
following:

283 Three-light window with six scenes
from the life of Christ and the Virgin, the
three upper scenes in each light being in
panels with lobed tops; centre scenes: (1) the
'Annunciation' taking place in a room, with
the Virgin in blue mantle kneeling on right
separated from Gabriel by scroll: 'ave gracia
plena dominus tecu(m)'; the Dove descends
in stream of light from bust of God the
Father top left in diapered red ground.
(2) 'Birth of the Virgin' with the child
standing on the red cover of a blue and
white curtained bed held by her mother
while a servant beckons and a midwife
washes linen in a tub; left hand scenes:
(3) 'Christ before Pilate' with the latter
enthroned in scarlet and ermine on the
right and Christ led bound between soldiers
and a noisy rabble, one of whom
brandishes bundles of reeds.
(4) 'Agony in the Garden' showing an angel
with cross and chalice appearing to Christ
in blue robe kneeling at the foot of a hillock
in front of three sleeping disciples within a
wattled enclosure; to the left Judas
directing a band of soliders; right hand
scenes: (5) the 'Resurrection' with Christ
facing in red holding banner stepping out
of the tomb between two angels; two guards
reclining in foreground; (6) 'Christ Appearing to St. Peter', the latter, seated beside a
rock, with raised hands and large key, and
Christ, with banner, in scarlet robe.
57¾ × 29in. (upper scenes); 43 × 29in.
(lower scenes). German, 2nd quarter, 15th
century. Ex Coll. Baron Pückler (acquired
1818); Friedrich Spitzer; Hearst. Exhib.

McLellan Galleries, Glasgow, 1951,
no.499. Lit: Wentzel, *Pantheon*,
September–October, 1961, p.244, pl.6.
(45.485).
After the secularisation of the Carmelite
convent by Napoleon, the church was taken
over by the town and the stained glass sold
in 1818 to Baron Pückler for an intended
chapel at his castle of Muskau. It remained,
however, in store until the Baron's death
in 1871, after which most of the glass was
acquired by Friedrich Spitzer in Paris.
One large window, or section of a window,
known as the 'Throne of Solomon',
remained at Muskau until its destruction
in the war in 1945. According to a report of
1877 the stained glass came from the
windows of the choir and the chief feature
of the most important window was an
'Adoration of the Virgin surrounded
by representations of the Ten
Commandments', but research has shown
that the windows, which are now chiefly
divided between the Burrell Collection and
the Metropolitan Museum, New York, all
came from the five windows in the north
aisle of the church, an extension to the
main body of the church begun in 1439
(see Jane Hayward, 'Stained Glass
Windows from the Carmelite Church at
Boppard-am-Rhein', *Metropolitan Museum
Journal*, vol.2, 1969). The Burrell
triple-light shown here with six scenes
from Christ's Passion and the life of the
Virgin once formed most of the lower half
of a rare variant of a Tree of Jesse window
(J. Dinkel, *Scottish Art Review*, vol. XIII,
no.2, 1971, pp.22–7). The existence of the
Jesse figure, now in a private collection in
the U.S.A., was first predicated by W.
Wells from the Spitzer Catalogue
Supplement (*Scottish Art Review*, vol.x.
no.3, 1966, pp.22–5).

Oriental Carpets

284 Persian arabesque carpet
Sefavid, 16th century
Wool pile, 11ft.5in. × 9ft.4in. (9.3)
The fluid arabesque pattern, chiefly in
pale blue is symmetrically disposed on a
golden yellow field around a well defined
central medallion within a deeper blue
border. Date of acquisition untraced.

285 Persian medallion carpet
(fragment)
16th century
Wool pile, 11ft.3in. × 5ft. (9.27)
A large medallion, with twig and leaf
filling, and shades of bluish-green between
the eight rays of the star, is superimposed
on a rose-red field, ornamented with
yellow scrolls terminating in arabesques.
Parts of a cartouche and pendant and one
corner cartouche remain (M. H. Beattie,
'The Burrell Collection of Oriental Rugs',
Oriental Art, VII, no.4, 1961, p.162).
Acquired 1936 (with a smaller fragment
from the same carpet).

286 Persian garden carpet
Sefavid, 17th century
Wool pile, 17ft.5in. × 14ft.2in. (9.2)
This famous carpet, known to have been
in Constantinople in the late 19th century,
was later in the Wagner Collection in
Berlin. For a time it was in the U.S.A.
whence it came to London by 1917, before
being acquired by J. A. Holms of Glasgow
from whose collection it was sold in
1938 (Morrison, McChlery, 17.10.38,
no.329). It was acquired by Sir William
the following year. The field shows a garden
scene with formal water channels and
central pool on a deep blue ground with
cypresses, plane and flowering trees. It was
probably woven in south Persia possibly
in Kerman to which vase carpets are
assigned. (A vase placed at either end of
the horizontal water course suggests that
this garden carpet may have had a similar
origin.) Since F. R. Martin discussed and

reproduced it in his history of Oriental
Carpets published in 1908 (p.81, fig.200)
it has frequently appeared in books and
articles; (see Beattie, 1961, p.165),

287 Persian lattice carpet (incomplete)
Sefavid, c.1600
Wool pile, 13ft.1in. × 3ft.4in. (9.7)
Strip comprising eleven complete lattices
and about as many incomplete ones from
the field of a floral lattice carpet, the
lattices composed of leaves each enclosing
a different flowering plant, one rising from
a vase, in a deep blue ground. (Beattie,
1961, p.164). Acquired 1916.

288 Persian tree carpet
c.1800
Wool pile, 11ft.4in. × 7ft.4in. (9.39)
A repeating pattern composed of five
alternating zones with cypress trees and
flowering plants in each; an incomplete
zone at the top indicates that the carpet
was originally larger. Formerly belonged
to Countess Ezapery Reningstein, near
Salzburg. Shown in the 'International
Exhibition of Persian Art', London, 1931,
Acquired 1936 (in Berlin).

289 Persian vase carpet
17th century
Wool pile, 11ft.9in. × 5ft.9in. (9.6)
The red field densely strewn with
flowering plants, two of which are in the
shape of vases, arranged in a symmetrical
but unobtrusive pattern (Beattie, 1961,
p.165). Formerly in the Steinkopf
Collection. Acquired 1935 (Christie's sale
of 23.5.35). The Collection contains nine
examples of Persian vase carpets.

290 Persian flowering plant carpet
17th century
Wool pile, 9ft.10in. × 6ft.5in. (9.5)
The red field almost totally obscured by an
even denser profusion of flowering plants.
Acquired 1935.

291 Caucasian dragon carpet
17th century
Wool pile, 16ft.7in. × 8ft. (9.38)
Within a lattice composed of bold
interlaced dark and light serrated leaves
are a number of paired and opposed motives
including the highly stylised dragons from
which this type of carpet is named; red
ground; narrow border with buff ground
(Beattie, 1961, pp.163–4). Acquired 1929.

292 Caucasian dragon carpet
18th century
Wool pile, 14ft.11in. × 6ft.3in. (9.42)
In this later example the ornamental
motives in yellow buff and blue on red,
have become much more highly stylised
and angular (Beattie, 1961, p.164).
Acquired 1932 (Sir John Ramsden Sale).

293 Indian animal carpet
c.1500
Wool pile, 8ft.9in. × 8ft.10in. (9.1)
This fragment in which birds and beasts,
some fabulous others quite naturalistic,
proliferate in a manner peculiar to Indian
symbolism is one of several fragments now
scattered among various museums in
France and America from a fantastic animal
carpet, probably the earliest existing
carpet of its kind (Beattie, 1961, p.162).
Said to have been formerly in the
Weininger Collection in Berlin, and later
in that of Loewenfeld in Paris. Acquired
1934 (from the Administration of the
Hapsburg Trust).

294 Indian animal carpet
17th century
Wool pile, 15ft.7in. × 6ft.7in. (9.32)
Various beasts, fabulous and otherwise,
including humped spotted cattle, kilins,
and tigers are shown in a red field dotted
with flowers in pursuit of deer and hares
within a green-blue border of wreathed
palmettes (Beattie, 1961, p.162). Formerly
belonged to the Earl of Mount Edgcumbe.
Acquired 1935.

295 Indian flowering plant carpet
17th century
Wool pile, 17ft.10in. × 6ft.3in. (9.35)
A repeating pattern of floral arabesques in a red field; border with palmettes in a blue ground (Beattie, 1961, p.162). Acquired 1937.

296 Indian flowering plant carpet
17th century
Wool pile, 11ft.4in. × 5ft.2in. (9.33)
The Indian version of a Persian flowering plant carpet with a far more insistent and symmetrically balanced design (Beattie, 1961, p.162). Acquired 1935.

297 Indian flowering plant carpet
17th century
Wool pile, 10ft.5in. × 5ft.2½in. (9.34)
Another example of an Indian carpet of the same type in which the design is even more crisply defined. Acquired 1935.

Chinese Ceramics and Bronzes

298 Neolithic burial urn*
Globular body, twin-loop handles; painted in black and purple with a trellis pattern enclosing diamonds and circles divided by a vertical stripe; 14¼in. high; 20in. dia.; from Kansu province in Honan (Yang-Shao culture). Acquired 1945 (Lionel Edwards sale). (38.1)
The trellis design is discussed by A. de Sowerby, *The China Journal*, vol.22, no.6. 1935, pp.300–03, repro. coloured frontispiece, fig.A.

299 Neolithic burial urn
Globular body; twin loop handles; cylindrical neck; painted in black and purple with spirals; 15½in. high; 17in. dia., from Kansu province in Honan (Yang-Shao culture). Acquired 1944 (N. S. Brown sale). (38.4)
For an account of the Kansu find see G. Anderssen, *Memoirs of the Geological Survey of China*, Series A, no.5, 1925.

300 Neolithic burial urn
Globular body; twin loop handles; painted in black and purple with large spirals; 13¼in. high; 16½in. dia.; from Kansu province in Honan (Yang-Shao culture). Acquired 1947. (38.5)

301 Neolithic burial urn*
Ovoid body; twin loop handles; painted in red and black with cruciform pattern; 12in. high; 13in. dia.; from Kansu province in Honan (Yang-Shao culture). Acquired 1948 (N. S. Brown sale). (38.12)
Reproduced by A. de Sowerby, 1935, frontispiece fig.B. During the 1940s Sir William acquired thirty-six examples of Kansu neolithic wares of which at least nineteen came directly or indirectly from the N.S. Brown Collection. They form the strongest collection in Britain.

302 Vase with felspathic 'ash' glaze and comma decoration
Ovoid with twin lug handles; 8¼in. high; 7¼in. dia.; Han Dynasty (206 B.C.–A.D. 220). Acquired 1947. (38.44)

303 Lead glazed granary tower
9¾in. high; 7½in. dia.: Han Dynasty. Acquired 1945 (ex. Johnston Collection). (38.79)
There are forty-seven pieces of Han lead-glazed wares in the Collection.

304 Cream glazed ewer with phoenix-head handle
14½in. high; 5in. dia.; T'ang Dynasty (618–906). Acquired 1931. (38.173)

305 Cream glazed bullock with halter and harness in low relief
7½in. high; 7½in. long; T'ang Dynasty. Acquired 1945. (38.127)
One of a pair.

306 Three colour glazed (striped and suffused) jar
7in. high; 5in. dia. (mouth); T'ang Dynasty Acquired 1947. (38.191)

307 Three colour glazed handled cup
2⅝in. high; 3⅜in. dia.; T'ang Dynasty. Acquired 1947. (38.210)
There are 35 pieces of T'ang coloured enamelled wares and 25 white ones in the Collection.

308 Covered jar with brown flocculent glaze
11in. high; 8¾in. dia.; T'ang Dynasty. Acquired 1945. (Mrs. C. G. Seligman sale). (38.227)

309 Ting yao (white ware) bowl
Rim sheathed in copper with six lobes and flower carved in the glaze in the centre; 2⅞in. high; 8⅜in. dia; Sung Dynasty (960–1279). Acquired 1944 (N. S. Brown sale). (38.266)

310 Yueh yao (green ware) vase and cover
Carved with lotus petals; 13¼in. high; 6¼in. dia. (at centre); early Sung (10th

century). Acquired 1943 (Sir A. Daniel Hall sale). (38.280)

311 Yueh Yao (green ware) bowl
Slightly lobed and with horizontal bands under the rim; 3½in. high; 8in. dia.; early Sung, c.1000. Formerly in the Eumorfopoulos Collection. Acquired 1943 (Sir A. Daniel Hall sale). (38.297)

312 Honan vase with screw mouth
Iron red flowers in brown glaze; 8½in. high; Sung, 12th century. Formerly in the Radcliffe Collection. Acquired 1948. (38.386)
There are thirty-eight Sung pieces in the Collection.

313 Korean celadon bowl
Copper red decoration both inside and out; 2½in. high; 7⅛in. dia. Koryu period, early 13th century. Formerly in the Ezekiel Collection. Acquired 1946. (38.302)
Another example of this rare type is in the British Museum (ex. Eumorfopoulos Collection).

314 Celadon ewer
Long spout and high strap handle; 12½in. high; 8in. dia.; Yuan Dynasty, 14th century. Acquired 1946 with another celadon ewer of similar shape and size. (38.306)

315 Ch'ing pai (misty blue) flower vase
Mei p'ing shape; decorated with dragons, lotus leaves and floral scroll; 10¾in. high: 6¼in. dia.; Yuan Dynasty, 14th century. (38.253)
Formerly in the Joshua Collection. Acquired 1945.
Unlike the only known comparable jar (Cleveland Museum of Art exhibition, 1968, no.99) Basil Gray notes that this vase has carved, as distinct from moulded, decoration.

316 Blue and white dish*
Serrated edges; decorated with banana, bamboo, gourd and peony; lotus pattern under the rim; 3in. high; 18¼in. dia.; 14th century. Acquired 1945. (38.658)
Belongs to rare group of pre-Ming 'blue

and white'. The Collection contains 34 pieces of the Yuan Dynasty, representing all the principal wares of the period, especially ch'ing pai and celadon. (See Basil Gray, 'The Development of Taste in Chinese Art in the West 1872 to 1972', *Transactions of the Oriental Ceramic Society*, 1974, pp.25–26).

317 Figure of a Lohan seated on a throne of rock
4ft.2in. high; 2ft.2½in. wide; reign of Ch'eng Hua (1465–1487). Acquired 1944. (38.419)
An inscription on the side reads:
'Ch'eng – hua twentieth year (1484) mid-autumn, made on an auspicious day. The believer, Wang Chinao, his wife Miao-chin and son Wang Ch'in and the priest Tao-chi, the workman Liu Chen' (translated by Roderick Whitfield, British Museum). Another large Buddhist figure bearing a date corresponding to 1484 is in the Victoria and Albert Museum and a companion figure is in the British Museum (see *British Museum Quarterly*, XI, 1937, p.112, pl.xxxix).

318 Fish bowl
Decorated in under-glaze blue and copper red with fishes among weeds; 18½in. high; 17½in. dia.; Ming Dynasty, late 16th century. Acquired 1947. (38.429)

319 Blue and white tankard with cover
Dragon handle; 7⅜in. high; 6in. dia.; Ming, probably reign of Yung Lo (1403–1424). Formerly in the A. F. Parfitt Collection. Acquired 1946. (38.443)

320 Pear-shaped ewer*
Decorated in underglaze copper-red with two ogival panels on the sides, a band of petals and a fret border round the foot, scroll borders and fern fronds round the neck; 12¾in. high; 8in. dia.; Ming, late 14th century. Acquired 1947. (38.455)
Lent to the exhibition of 'The Arts of the Ming Dynasty', organised by the Oriental Ceramic Society in the Arts Council Gallery, November–December, 1957, cat. no.150.

321 Fa-hua (cloisonné-style decoration) bulb bowl
Lotuses on purple ground; 3¾in. high; 7in. dia.; Ming, 16th century. Acquired 1945. (38.536)

322 Fa-hua wine jar
Kuan form; cloisonné decoration of cranes and peonies between tasseled ornament above and panelling round base in dark blue ground; 12½in. high; 6½in. dia; Ming, 15th century. Acquired 1942. (38.546)
There are 30 examples of Fa hua wares in the Collection, one of the finest in the British Isles.

Bronzes

323 Wine goblet (chueh) for pouring libations
Loop handle with monster mask; tao tieh decoration on sides below cicada pattern; inscribed character under handle; 7⅜in. high; 6⅜in. wide; Shang-yin Dynasty, 13th to 14th century B.C. Acquired 1942. (8.15)
The twin projections with caps rising from the lips of ritual wine vessels of this type are thought to be for lifting with tongs when the wine was heated in them.

324 Wine bucket (Yu) with swing handle*
Bulbous body with ornamental band containing archaic long tailed birds in relief; handles terminate in deer heads; inscription of three characters cast inside body ('sacred vessel made for travelling'); 8¼in. high; 8¼in. wide; the cover is a reproduction; Western Chou Dynasty, 11th century B.C. Acquired 1945 (Lionel Edwards sale). (8.2)
The cover of vessels of this type is intended to serve as a goblet.

325 Food vessel (Kuei) with two loop handles
Exterior decorated with broad band of bosses between narrower bands of fret divided at the top by rams' heads; dragon head masks on the handles; inscription of

two characters inside; 7in. high; 12¾in. wide; Chou Dynasty, 11th century B.C. Acquired 1947 (Henry Brown sale). (8.3)

326 Food vessel (Kuei) with two loop handles
Exterior decorated with broad band of tao tieh masks between split dragon borders divided under the rim by rams' heads; bovine masks on handles; smooth water patina; 5¼in. high; 11¼in. wide; Chou Dynasty, 10th century B.C. Acquired 1943. (8.4)

327 Food vessel (Fu) and reversible cover of similar shape*
Both with two monster mask loop handles and relief decoration of dragon motives and scrolling border; on the rim are four lugs for keeping the cover in position; 7in. high; 11⅜in. wide; Chou Dynasty, 6th to 5th century B.C. (8.43)
This bronze, described by Professor Yetts as 'very important piece' seems to have been among Sir William's early purchases. Between 1911 and 1918 he acquired over seventy Chinese bronzes, but most of his important pieces were bought after 1940.

328 Tripod wine vessel (Li-ting)*
With loop handle disgorged by bovine head; double raised ring round neck under projecting lip; inscription under handle; water patina; 9¾in. high; 6⅛in. dia. (at mouth); Chou Dynasty, early 10th century B.C. Acquired 1950. (8.164)
A very rare type of wine vessel.

329 Small tripod water dropper
Globular body with spout resembling crested turtle head and neck; loop handle and hinged lid; pale green patina; 3¼in. high; 4¾in. wide; Han Dynasty (204 B.C.–A.D. 220). Acquired 1947 (Henry Brown sale). (8.167)

330 Large cylindrical vessel (lien)*
Supported on three feet in the form of three naked kneeling men; flanged rim for missing cover; at equidistant points round the body are four ring handles attached to animal masks; between three bands of

horizontal fluting are four zones of low relief decoration, geometrical at top and bottom, and animal motives in the two central ones; 20¼in. high; 22½in. dia.; probably from Shih Chai Shan, Yunnan, 3rd–2nd century B.C. From a French private collection. Acquired 1948. (8.170)
A group of related bronzes are in the British Museum.

Antiquities

331 Sumerian stone head of statuette
Half life-sized, bald male with single raised eye-brow and large eye-sockets; back of head and shoulders missing; alabaster 5in. high; early Dynastic III, c.2600–2400 B.C. Acquired 1948. (28.5)

332 Neo-Sumerian foundation figure
Standard nail type carrying basket on head; largely effaced inscription on skirt; copper; 10¾in. long; third Dynasty of Ur, c.2113–2006 B.C. Acquired 1955. (28.75)
Such foundation figures have been found in brick boxes, sealed inside with bitumen, usually at the sides of gateways or at the corners of temples. This example allegedly came from Uruk in South Mesopotamia.

333 Babylonian (?) terra-cotta lion head*
Perhaps part of a near life-sized figure; snarling, the whiskers looping from the nose and the mane in the shape of slanting and incised ribs; traces of red paint in the eyes and mouth; greenish-white clay; Isin-Larsa period, c.2000–1800 B.C. Acquired 1950. (28.37)
Probably the head of a protecting lion like those at the entrance to the temple of Nisaba at Harinal. Other clay examples, probably from the same source as the Burrell one, are in the Louvre.

334 Neo-Assyrian fragment of stone relief slab
Two scribes facing right tallying goods beneath a palm tree; both hold a stylus between thumb and clenched hand, and in their left hands small, hinged diptychs; marble; 7¼in. × 6in.; Sinnacherib-Ashurbanipal, 704–627 B.C. Acquired 1947 (28.33)
Scribes are characteristically rendered in pairs, but this representation is unusual in that both scribes hold tablets whereas normally one is shown with a reed pen

and scroll, writing Aramaic. The palm indicates a Southern (Babylonian?) setting and the style of hair a 7th century date. Hinged note books of the type shown have been found at Nimrud.

335 Neo-Assyrian fragment of stone relief slab
Head of an Assyrian soldier amongst palm (?) trees; long, square cut, beard, curled moustache, pointed helmet with ear guards; marble 6in. × 4in.; Sinnacherib, 704–681 B.C. Acquired 1952 (28.65)
Probably from the South-West palace at Nineveh.

336 Urartian bull's head cauldron protome
Socketed; the hair in flat relief between oval incised eye-brows and eyes; bronze; 5¾in. × 4½in.; late 8th–early 7th centuries B.C. Acquired in April 1957. (33.212)
This head is almost identical with two others in the British Museum known to come from Rassam's excavations of Toprak Kale (Lake Van), Turkey, in 1880. A fourth one is in the Walter's Art Gallery Baltimore. A complete cauldron from another site shows four bulls' heads attached to a flat wing and tailpiece riveted near the rim. (*Scottish Art Review*, vol.6, no.4, 1958, pp.27–8.)
The last addition Sir William made to his collection of ancient antiquities.

337 Semi-circular bowl with in-curving lip
Dark grey mottled stone (?granite); 7¾in. high × 13½in. dia.; probably early dynastic. Acquired 1948. (13.1)

338 Oblate bowl with two lug handles and flattened rim*
Black and white speckled breccia; 6¾in. high × 3⅞in. dia. (at mouth); predynastic, Gerzean period. Acquired 1948. (13.2)

339 Oblate bowl with lug side handles with open slits
Wide flattened rim; black and white breccia; 4⅝in. high × 9¾in. dia.; early dynastic. Acquired 1948. (13.3)

Slits said to be for attachment of rope handles.

340 Semi-ovoid bowl with flattened base
Red and white mottled breccia; 5⅞in. high × 7¼in. dia.; predynastic. Acquired 1948. (13.28)

341 Flattened oblate bowl with two lug handles and flattened rim
Mottled breccia; 8½in. high × 13¼in. wide; predynastic, Gerzean period. Acquired 1948. (13.89)

342 Ovoid bowl with two lug handles and raised lip
Speckled black and white breccia; 8¼in. high × 7½in. dia.; predynastic, Gerzean period. Acquired 1948. (13.97)
The manufacture of multicoloured vessels of hard stone is said to have originated during the fourth Millenium B.C. at the edge of the Upper Egyptian Nile Valley and in the mountains of the Eastern Desert. The earliest ones predate the first stone reliefs and statues.

343 Egyptian (Old Kingdom) coloured relief fragment*
Youth holding offering of goose and a covered jar; limestone; 12½in. × 15½in.; Sixth Dynasty (2423–2263 B.C.). Acquired 1955. (13.279)

344 Egyptian (Middle Kingdom) torso from a pair of statues
He still grasps the hand of his missing wife; limestone; 8½in. high; Eighteenth Dynasty (2nd phase) 1450–1372 B.C. Acquired 1954. (13.251)

345 Egyptian (Saite) figure of an ibis
Bronze; 6in. × 7in.; 26th Dynasty (663–525 B.C.). Acquired 1953. (13.247)

346 Late Mycenaen two-handled stem cup
Red concentric decoration round base, stem and lower part of bowl; the upper part decorated with repeating pattern of broad strokes and hatching; 7¼in. high; 12th century B.C. Acquired 1948. (19.28)

347 Late Mycenean two-handled stem cup
Red concentric decoration round base, stem and lower part of bowl; the upper part decorated with running loops; 7in. high; 13th century B.C. Acquired 1950. (19.96)

348 Corinthian jug (oinochoe) with trefoil lip
Squat body with flat base; painted in reddish brown with concentric bands containing friezes of animals and birds in a rosette-scattered ground; 6¾in. high × 6in. dia.; c.650 B.C. Acquired 1950. (19.137)

349 Corinthian pot (aryballos)
Black figured decoration including two confronted harpies; 6in. high; c.600–580 B.C. Acquired 1952. (19.105)

350 Corinthian bronze helmet with nose and cheek protectors
Chased border decoration; 8⅜in. high; 6th century B.C. Acquired 1948. (19.60)

351 Attic black-figured pottery amphora*
On the sides a walking lion in a reserved panel; 14in. high; 570–550 B.C. Acquired 1947. (19.10)

352 Attic black-figured pottery cup (Kotyle)
Frieze of two men and a dog chasing a hare; 5⅛in. dia.; c.550 B.C. Acquired 1952. (19.108)

353 South Italian feeding bottle (askos) in form of a pig
Painted brown decoration of dots and dashes; two pierced dorsal flanges for suspension; 7in. long; late 4th century B.C. Acquired 1949. (19.65)

354 Greek marble head of goddess
Much worn and nose partly missing; the hair parted in middle and bound with a fillet; the size of the head indicates a more than life-size statue; 11in. high; fourth century B.C. Acquired 1948. (19.58)

355 Greek terra-cotta figure of a Bacchic Eros

Figure looking down with one hand making upward, the other downward movement; drapery hangs over right arm and left shoulder; traces of red painted decoration; 8¼in. high; third century B.C.; perhaps made at Myrina in Asia Minor, where hundreds of clay statuettes have been found and Eros was a popular subject. Acquired 1955. (19.161)

356 Greek (or Roman?) porphyry head of a god

The head bound with a double pig-tail, a hair style generally adopted by Greek youths at the beginning of the 5th century B.C.; the fringe and beard, separated into rippling strands curling at the ends, fall in four (originally five) stages; the left side and back are missing; 13¾in. high; probably Roman copy of the 1st or 2nd century A.D. of a Zeus or Poseidon of the second quarter of the 5th century B.C. Acquired by Sir William in 1950 as a Byzantine porphyry head of an emperor of the 5th century A.D. (Inv. 95)
More recent opinion is divided as to whether it is a Roman copy or a Greek original. Last year it was published as the work of the Spartan sculptor, Pythagoras, who, the author believes, carried out the pediment sculptures for the Temple of Olympia. (Jose Dörig, 'Der Zeus von Glasgow', *Neue Zurcher Zeitung*, 16/17 November 1974, Nr. 493, S. 69).

357 Bronze torso of youth

Head tilted and gaze directed downward; curling hair parted in middle; eye sockets hollow; traces of brown patination and red pigment; both arms missing from below shoulders; body fractured at waist; 16½in. high; probably Roman copy of the late 1st century B.C. or early 1st century A.D. of a Greek original of the 5th century B.C. in the style of Polycleitos. Acquired (19.162)

Mediaeval Antiquities

358 Stone roundel*

Within a circular border of foliage; standing in a rowing boat three men, two bearded, one clean shaven, are casting the body of a naked youth, a millstone suspended from his neck, into the sea; a fourth boatman on the right holds the rudder; 14½in. dia.; French c.1260. Acquired in 1946 when it was described as English, mid 15th century and as depicting the casting of St. Clement into the sea. (44.38)
St. Clement however is usually depicted as a bishop being cast into the sea with an anchor, not a millstone, hanging from his neck, and the carving is obviously far earlier and probably French. Of the three saints cast into the sea with a millstone, St. Quirinus, St. Callixtus and St. Vincent, the latter seems to be the most likely, for his life and martyrdom formed the subject of several important cycles in the 12th and 13th centuries, especially in stained glass at St. Denis, Angers, Rouen, Chartres and St. Germain-des-Prés. St. Vincent, bishop of Saragosa, was persecuted in the reigns of Diocletian and Maximian. After martyrdom his corpse was thrown into the sea by sailors who, on their return, found that it had already been miraculously washed up on the shore. The roundel may originally have formed a boss at the intersection of vaulting ribs.

359 Stone figure of a standing saint

Wearing a blue dress girdled high above the waist and a red mantle; both forearms missing; the face is youthful, serious and unsmiling; limestone; 35in. high; French; 1250–1300. Acquired in 1938 at the George Durlacher sale as a French female saint without any indication of date. (44.18)
Wentzel points out (*Pantheon* XX, 1, 1962, S.2–7) it is impossible to say for certain whether a male or female is intended. In 13th century statues of young girls the hair is usually longer and noble and married women wear headcloths. It is even possible that the figure was originally provided with wings as an angel, perhaps holding a candlestick or shield.

360 Stone equestrian figure

Said to depict St. Martin dividing his cloak; wearing armour on a caparisoned horse; left fore-arm and whole of right arm missing, also right leg; 28in. × 22in.; probably Flemish, c.1450. Acquired 1932 from Miss Steel (Andrade) as French, 14th century stone group. (44.15)

361 Stone bust of an armoured man

Hands pressed together in prayer; 26in. high; French, 15th century. Acquired 1929 as a 15th century stone bust of Le Chevalier Dunois. (44.25)
Jean d'Orléans, Count of Dunois and Longeville (1402–1468), called the Bastard of Orléans, was the natural son of Louis, brother of Charles VI of France. He joined forces with Joan of Arc during the Siege of Orléans and expelled the English. Whether intended to represent him or not the bust would appear to derive from a kneeling life-sized figure.

362 Stone figure of a standing shepherd

Wearing hooded garment with cape and girdle; looking upward with a bundle attached to his back; 31in. high; French or Flemish, 15th century. Date of acquisition untraced. (44.26)
The figure presumably formed part of a group representing the annunciation of the Nativity to the Shepherds.

363 Stone figure of the Virgin and Child

Crowned; wearing red under dress with laced bodice under a deep blue mantle; the child in loose green robe; left arm and right fore-arm of the child missing; 36in. high; French, 15th century. Acquired 1931. (44.5)

364 Stone pair of flying angels

Heads with long hair bound with fillets; bodies enveloped in girdled tunics; one hand of each angel holds the remains of a broken object, possibly a candle; traces of pigment on eyes and mouths; top of wings missing; 17in. high; French or Flemish, 15th century. Acquired 1929 in France as 'statuettes en pierre polychromée representant deux anges'. (44.22 and 23) Flying, and apparently grieving, angels such as these sometimes appear in conjunction with a crucified Christ holding chalices beneath the bleeding hands of the Saviour, but the hands of these angels are not sufficiently outstretched for that function, nor do the fragments of the object they hold suggest the stem of a chalice.

365 Stone figure of St. Barbara
Holding palm and book; wearing square cut bodice, a robe with traces of blue pigment and a mantle with traces of red, probably originally provided with a tower, which is her most usual attribute; inscribed 'St. Barbe' on pedestal; 39in. high; French or Flemish, c.1520. Acquired 1935 (44.17)

366 Alabaster carving depicting the Throne of Mercy
God the Father enthroned holds a napkin containing the souls of the saved above the crucified Christ; 35in. high; English, 1375–1380. Acquired 1938. (Inv.19) In a review of an exhibition of British mediaeval art to which it was lent the following year, Sir Nikolaus Pevsner wrote: 'Of late gothic sculpture the best examples shown are alabaster work, above all God the Father with the Crucified Son and the souls of the saved ('Gnadenstuhl') from Sir William Burrell's Collection . . .' (*Burlington Magazine*, July 1959, p.14). The subject, for which the literary source is Hebrews Chap.4, v.16, occurs as early as the 12th century in art. A very similar 14th century alabaster from Abergavenny Church is in the Victoria and Albert Museum but the head of God the Father is missing; another fine example of similar date and iconography, but with the addition of two small kneeling donor

figures is in the Boston Museum of Fine Arts. God the Father enthroned in a niche holding the souls of the saved is represented as part of the Last Judgement carved above the central door of the west facade at Bourges Cathedral.

367 Wood figure of a kneeling woman
Turned to left with hands raised; fashionably dressed in the costume of the period with turban-type headdress and wimple, close fitting bodice and ample skirt, painted in colour and gold; 14½in. high; Flemish, 15th century. (50.49) Acquired 1923 as 'statuette of a kneeling saint in carved polychrome work'. Possibly she originally represented one of the mid-wives in a Flemish retable of the first half of the 15th century depicting the Nativity.

368 Carved wood group depicting the Lamentation (Pietà)*
The body of Christ half-raised is supported by St. John while the Virgin holds his limp arm and gazes at his face; on the right a fashionably attired St. Mary Magdalen nervously fingers her ointment jar; well preserved polychrome paint work; 3ft.7in. × 3ft.6in.; South German, c.1500. Formerly in the Oertel Collection, Munich (cat. 1913, pl.24, p.39). Acquired 1938 (from the collection of the Brooklyn Museum). (50.96) Strictly speaking a Pietà represents the dead Christ in the arms of his mourning mother alone, but sometimes, as here, other figures are included (*Scottish Art Review*, vol. XIV, no.1, 1973, p.16, repro. in colour).

369 Carved and painted wood figure of a standing musician
Playing portable organ with five pipes; apparently male, wearing girdled tunic and shoulder length hair; 22in. high; French or Flemish, 15th century. Acquired 1931, with its pair cat. no.370 described as 'bois sculpte angels playing musical instruments'. (50.62)

370 Carved and painted wood figure of a standing musician
Playing lute; youthful with shoulder length curly hair bound with fillet; wearing girdled tunic; 22in. high; French or Flemish, 15th century. Acquired 1931. (50.63) Pair of cat. no.369.

371 Bronze mount with three soldiers known as the 'Temple Pyx'*
Each soldier holding a kite-shaped shield is shown in high relief standing in front of an arcade of three round-topped arches; 3⅝in. × 2¾in.; perhaps German, c.1150. Formerly in the collections of Crofton Croker, Lord Londesborough and General Pitt-Rivers. Acquired 1936. (5 and 6.139) First discussed in the *The Gentleman's Magazine* (October, 1833, vol.103, p.305), this fragment, which may originally have been associated with an ecclesiastical container of some kind perhaps in the form of the Holy Sepulchre, is said to have been discovered in the Temple Church, London, during repairs having it is supposed been brought there by the Templars from their old church. A slightly smaller fragment in the Wallace Collection, London, with a single soldier holding a spear is very similar in style and probably from the same workshop. (T. D. Kendrick, 'The Temple Pyx', *Antiquaries Journal*, vol. XVI 1936, p.51–54). According to Kendrick this is most likely to have been in Germany; Zarnecki (*Burlington Magazine*, December, 1959, p.452) considers an English origin possible. It may however have been made in the Netherlands like the so-called reliquary in the Germanisches Museum, Nuremberg, in which the Holy Sepulchre, guarded by seated angels, is flanked by similar round-arched arcades under a sloping roof surmounted by the Descent from the Cross. The Holy Sepulchre thus formed is mounted on a rectangular container on one side of which is engraved the three sleeping soldiers wearing conical helmets, chain mail and holding kite-shaped

shields. It is attributed to Maastricht, c.1100.

372 Enamelled copper gilt chasse*
With a scene of the murder of Thomas à Beckett; the copper plates are mounted on a solid oak core; champleve enamel with some heads in relief (one missing); 6¾in. high; 4¾in. wide; France (Limoges), c.1200–1205. Formerly in the Thomas Barnet (?Barret); Horace Walpole; and Leopold Hirsch Collections. Acquired 1934. (Inv.6)
This historic reliquary was first noted and drawn by William Cole in 1762 in the fortieth volume of his MS Collections now in the British Museum (Add. MS. 5841.149 p.151) describing the curiosities at Strawberry Hill; 'In the same collection is a most curious and venerable piece of antiquity in enamel on copper, representing the model of the Shrine of St. Thomas of Canterbury . . . It stands upon 4 awkward square feet and has a gothic ornament at top with 3 balls on it . . .' It is recorded in the Strawberry Hill sale catalogue (1842), p.137, no.83: 'A model of the shrine of Thomas à Beckett, a very singular specimen of the old English enamel, which is now exceeding rare'. (See also T. Borenius, 'Some Further Aspects of the Iconography of St. Thomas of Canterbury', *Archaeologia* vol.83, 1933, p.197, pl. XLVI).

373 Bronze candlestick
In the form of a man with long hair riding a lion; engraved details; traces of gilding in crannies; 12¼in. high; 7¼in. wide; Mosan (? Dinant) 13th century. Formerly in the collections of Bardac, von Frey, and Hearst. Acquired 1939. (5 and 6.26)
This work was acquired together with another of similar type in which the figure kneeling on the back of the lion with one hand in its jaws conforms more closely with the biblical text (Judges, Chap. 14, v.6) describing the slaying of the lion by Samson. Both were described and reproduced by Falke and Meyer in their standard work (1935) on gothic candelabra (*Die Romanische Leuchter und Gefässer der Gotik*, nos. 254 and 255, abb. 218, 219)

when the one shown was still in the Sigismund Bardac Collection in Paris. The authors in fact singled out this candlestick as the 'Paradestück der Gattung' ('The masterpiece of its kind').

374 Enamelled copper gilt pyx*
In the shape of a dove; standing on a roundel with three branches for suspension; the wings and tails bear champleve enamel decoration and are movable; the back is fitted with a hinged cover; 7½in. long; French (Limoges), 2nd quarter of the 13th century. Acquired 1950. (Inv.27)
Pyxes in the shape of a Eucharistic dove as a container for the reserved sacraments during the celebration of mass seem to first date from the 10th century and several examples dating from the 12th and 13th centuries survive. The stand was used for suspension over the altar by a chain or rope, sometimes in association with a pulley so that the pyx could be lowered when required.

375 Bronze aquamanile*
In the form of a lion statant, the tail joined to the handle which resembles a coursing whippet; the handle and flattened area between head and mane bear Hebrew inscriptions; 11¾in. high; 13in. wide; German (?Lubeck), 1st half 14th century. Acquired 1938 (Mortimer Schiff sale). (5 and 6.9)
According to Falke and Meyer (*Bronzgeräte des Mittelalters*, p.114, no.480, Abb.447) this aquamanile came from a synagogue in Brilon-in-Westphalia and the inscriptions relate to the passover service for which it was used.

376 Ivory panel from a diptych
Four scenes in two registers (1) the Flagellation; (2) Crucifixion; (3) Virgin and Child between St. John the Baptist and St. Catherine; (4) St. George, depicted in high relief beneath an arcading and separated by columns. 6 7/16 in. × 4⅞in.; French, 14th century. Acquired 1947. (21.9)

In 1967 it was proved that this panel was the left wing of a diptych, of which the right wing was acquired by the British Museum in 1885. The four scenes on the latter show the 'Resurrection' and the 'Maries at the Sepulchre' in the upper register and St. Martin and two seated saints in the lower and on the back is inscribed in an 18th century hand: 'Found with its fellow under an old hog's trough near Mansfield in Nottinghamshire. Given me by my uncle, Doct. Pinkney'. After the separation, the Burrell panel was replaced by a cedar wood panel of the same size (now missing) on which an inscription stated that the diptych came from the Grange near Grantham, home of the Bury family and later of the Fisher family from whom the estate was purchased by the Duke of Rutland (d.1772). (*Scottish Art Review*, vol. XI, no.1, 1967, pp. 26–28).

377 Ivory mirror case
Scene of a couple playing chess under a draped tent; the periphery ornamented with four grotesques, two with male and two with female faces; 3¼in. dia.; French, 1st half 14th century. Formerly in the Cardon Collection, Brussels. Acquired 1947. (21.11)
As Koechlin (*Les Ivoires gothiques français*, vol. II, no.1055) noted, this ivory which is traversed vertically through the centre by a dark stain about 1 in. wide, must have been scorched by fire at some time. A very similar mirror case, also with four figures, is in the Louvre (Koechlin no.1053).

378 Drinking horn with silver gilt mounts
Steeply curving ox horn mounted on three feet, the two front ones having kneeling wild-men supporters; a conical tail piece is surmounted by a turret from which emerges a nude female figure holding an inscribed scroll; the lip band is inscribed: 'Jhesus autem tranciens per medium illoru(m) ibat' (St. John XX, 26: 'Then came Jesus and stood in the midst of them'); the medial band is inscribed in Latin:

'Jhesus maria Johanus Anna; it also has a small black letter inscription in German on the under side: 'her cord durekop heft my ghegeue(n) to eyner dechtny(s)' (Mr. Cord Durekop has given me (this cup) as a memorial): 10½in. high; 11in. wide; North Germany, 15th–16th century. Acquired 1941 (43.12).

Comparable drinking horns are to be seen in north Germany and Scandinavia and this provenance is confirmed by the German inscription which, according to Dr. Léonie von Wilkens has peculiarities which point in the same direction.

379 Ivory cup with silver gilt mounts

Straight sided cylindrical bowl with raised band between three incised lines; squat moulded stem and foot; the rim and base mounted in silver gilt engraved with running foliage; 5 3/16 in. high; 3½in. dia.; English c.1580. Acquired 1937. (43.11)

Tudor 'font-shaped' cups, of which another more famous example is the Howard Grace Cup in the Victoria and Albert Museum, London, have been discussed at length by N. M. Penzer, in *Apollo* (1957, vol.66, pp.174–179; 1958, vol.67, pp.44–49, and pp.82–86).

380 Rectangular box covered with bone plaques

Carved in low relief with hunting and other scenes in a hatched ground and the wood base marked out in squares as a chess board; in the corners of the lid are four armorial shields, of which the two upper ones might represent the Counts of Würtemberg who, from 1419 to 1480, bore a shield charged with three antlers impaling two fishes addorsed for Mumpelgard; 3 in. high; 7in. long; perhaps Middle Rhenish, c.1470. Acquired 1935. (21.19)

The box belongs to a well-known group of caskets usually ascribed to North Italy, although Koechlin (nos.1317–1328) considers them to be French (possibly North-eastern). The heraldic shields on this box, the only one known to bear armorial

evidence, seems however to point to the Middle Rhineland (see P. Beard, 'Arms on Fifteenth Century Box', *The Connoisseur*, 1935, vol.96, p.238).

381 Set of three silver gilt standing cups with steeple top covers

Conical bowls chased with carnations, tulips and strapwork; vase shaped-stems with scroll-handles; tall waisted bases; largest cup: 19 3/16 in. high; two smaller ones: 18in. high; English, 1611–12. Formerly in the Collections of Sir Samuel Montagu; Lord Acton; Lord Swaythling; Randolph Hearst. Acquired 1939. (43.16–18)

Each cup bears the same London hall-marks stamped both on the side of the bowl and on the cover for the year 1611–12, and the same maker's mark (TB in monogram), showing they belong together as a set, which is in fact the only set of three known, although over 70 separate existing ones have been recorded and of these over half were made between 1604 and 1615. In Elizabethan literature the obelisk is a symbol of the sovereignty of princes and it has been suggested that the vogue for these cups surmounted by a steeple or obelisk flourished during the stable rule of James I but tended to disappear as the authority of the Crown diminished. Doubtless this set was commissioned for a particular occasion, like the Richard Chester cup in the Victoria and Albert Museum which commemorated his term of office as master of Trinity House (see N. M. Penzer, 'The Steeple Cup IV', *Apollo*, October 1960, p.110, fig.9).

382 Hawking furniture

Pouch, glove, lure, and two hoods; the pouch made of two shaped leather panels with gold and enamelled mount is, like the glove, embroidered in metal and coloured threads with a tree and branching pattern of flowering and fruiting blackberry and mistletoe; the lure, richly ornamented with gold thread on blue velvet, is unlikely to have originally

belonged with the glove and pouch and has a more oriental flavour; pouch 17in. wide; glove 15in. long; lure 12in. long; ? English, early 17th century. From Wroxton Abbey; later in the Collection of Percival Griffiths. Acquired 1934. (29.151)

Said to have been given by James I to Lord Dudley North after the King had visited Wroxton to stand godfather to one of the North children. Wroxton, however, was owned by Sir William Pope, Bt., later Earl of Downe during the reign of James I, whose visit to the house is attested by a stained and painted window panel (now in the Royal Scottish Museum, Edinburgh) inscribed: 'Icy dans cette chambre coucha nostre Roy Jacques, premier de nom, le 23me Aoust 1619'. The king is recorded as having been entertained 'with the fashionable and courtly diversions of hawking and bear baiting'. (*The Connoisseur*, October, 1962, p.105).

Table of Sir William Burrell's acquisitions on page 48.

Heavy line between 1943/44 indicates the date the Collection was given to Glasgow.

Brackets enclose the number of objects entered in the records in the year indicated but which had been previously acquired.

Table of Sir William Burrell's acquisitions between 1911 and 1957 (see pages 6–11 and 47)

Bibliography

Articles and Publications dealing wholly or in part with aspects of The Burrell Collection

Glasgow Museums and Art Galleries: Annual Reports, 1944 to date (illustrated surveys with sections devoted to each Department including The Burrell Collection, describing main work and activities during the year).

Glasgow Art Gallery, *The Burrell Collection* 1949 – Seven picture booklets dealing with (1) *Ancient Civilisations*, (2) *Chinese Pottery*, (3) *Chinese Porcelain*, (4) *Tapestries*, (5) *Silver*, (6) *Pictures*, (7) *French Pictures*.

'Sir William Burrell', *Dictionary of National Biography*, *1951–1960*, pp.161–3.

W. Wells, 'Sir William Burrell's Purchase Books', *Scottish Art Review*, vol.9, no.2, 1963, pp.19–22. (Reprinted in *The English as Collectors* by Frank Herrman, 1972, pp.413–17).

W. Wells, 'Heraldic Art and The Burrell Collection', *The Connoisseur*, September, 1962, pp.3–11; October, 1962, pp.100–5.

W. Wells, 'Sir William Burrell and his Collection', *Museums Journal*, vol.72, no.3, December 1972, pp.101–3.

G. Seligman, *Merchants of Art 1880–1960*, 1961, pp.200–3.

D. Burrell, *Burrell's Straths: Fleet History of Burrell and Son, Glasgow*, unpublished manuscript, 1975.

'Burrell Collection Competition', *Architects' Journal*, 22 March 1972, pp.590–602, and 29 March 1972, pp.642–4.

B. Gasson, 'Notes on the Building for The Burrell Collection', *Museums Journal*, vol.72, no.3, December 1972, pp.104–6.

Ancient Civilisations

Various articles and notices in *Archiv für Orientforschung*, XV, 1945–51, pp.137–8; XVI (1), 1952, pp.112–13; XVI (2), 1953, pp.349–51; XVII (1), 1954–55, pp.185–6; XVII (2), 1956, pp.407–9; XVIII (1), 1957, pp.164–5; XVIII (2), 1958, pp.279–87 and p.438.

G. A. Burland, 'On an Oil Lacquered Gourd from Ancient Mexico', *Scottish Art Review*, vol.7, no.2, 1959, pp.26–7.

J. Dörig, 'Der Zeus von Glasgow', *Neue Zürcher Zeitung* (Literatur und Kunst Supplement), Nr. 493, 16/17 November 1974, p.69.

E. J. Peltenburg, *Catalogue of Western Asiatic Antiquities in The Burrell Collection* (in preparation).

J. G. Scott, 'Egyptian Stone Vases in The Burrell Collection', *Scottish Art Review*, vol.2, no.4, 1949, pp.25–7.

W. Wells, 'Bull's Head from Armenia', *Scottish Art Review*, vol.6, no.4, 1958, pp.27–8.

Chinese Art

B. Gray, 'The Development of Taste in Chinese Art in the West 1872 to 1972', *Transactions of the Oriental Ceramic Society*, 1974, pp.25–6.

A. Hannah, 'Chinese Pottery and Porcelain in The Burrell Collection', *Scottish Art Review*, vol.2, no.4, 1949, pp.16–21.

Persian Art

M. H. Beattie, 'The Burrell Collection of Oriental Rugs', *Oriental Art*, vol. 7, no.4, 1961, pp.162–9.

Glasgow Art Gallery and Museum, *Carpets and Tapestries from The Burrell Collection*, 1969.

European Art

TAPESTRIES

E. A. B. Barnard and A. J. B. Wace, 'The Sheldon Tapestry Weavers and their Work', *Archaeologia*, vol.78, 1928, pp.256–314.

D. P. Bliss, 'Tapestries in The Burrell Collection', *Scottish Art Review*, vol.2, no.4, 1949, pp.2–7.

G. H. Bushnell, 'Peruvian Textiles in The Burrell Collection', *Scottish Art Review*, vol.8, no.1, 1961, pp.22–5.

Comte Élie de Comminges, 'Une Tapisserie aux Armes, Beaufort, Turenne et Comminges', *Revue de Comminges* LXXXV, 1972, pp.267–290.

Jules Guiffrey, 'Tapisseries de l'Histoire de Saint Pierre', *Collection Paul Blanchot*, Paris, 1913, pp.60–4.

Glasgow Art Gallery and Museum, *Carpets and Tapestries from The Burrell Collection*, 1969.

A. F. Kendrick, 'Gothic Tapestries for Hutton Castle', *Country Life*, no.1584, 28 May, 1927, p.48a.

A. F. Kendrick, 'A Tapestry Altar Frontal of the 15th Century', *Burlington Magazine*, November 1926, p.211.

B. Kurth, 'Masterpieces of Gothic Tapestry in The Burrell Collection', *The Connoisseur*, March 1946, pp.3–12.

B. Kurth, 'Vier Unbekannte Schweizer Bildwirkereien', *Pantheon*, 1931, p.234.

B. Kurth, 'Eine Unbekannte Basler Bildwirkerei des 15ten Jahrhunderts', *Anzeiger für schweizerische Altertumskunde*, 2, 1938, p.146.

B. Kurth, 'A Middle Rhenish Bible Tapestry', *Burlington Magazine*, November 1939, pp.210–13.

B. Kurth, 'A Tapestry with the Death of Hercules', *Journal of the Warburg and Courtauld Institutes*, vol.5, 1942, p.241.

B. Kurth, 'Some Hitherto Unknown Tapestries with the Story of Jonathon Maccabeus', *The Connoisseur*, September 1947, p.22.

H. C. Marillier, 'An Ancient Tapestry Fragment', *Burlington Magazine*, September 1929, p.139.

H. C. Marillier, 'Sir William Burrell's Tapestry Fragment', *The Archaeological Journal*, 93, 1936, p.45.

J. K. Steppe and G. Delmarcel, 'Les Tapisseries du Cardinal Erard de la Marck, Prince-Évêque de Liège', *Revue de L'Art*, no.25, 1974, pp.41–2.

C. E. Tattersall, 'Sir William Burrell's Gothic Tapestries', *Old Furniture*, July 1927, pp.111–121.

W. Wells, 'The Seven Sacraments Tapestry – A New Discovery', *Burlington Magazine*, March 1959, pp.97–105.

W. Wells, 'Stories of the Tapestries', *Scottish Field*, December 1957.

W. Wells, 'A Burrell Tapestry', *Glasgow Herald*, 30 May 1959.

W. Wells, 'Two Tapestries in The Burrell Collection', *Scottish Art Review*, vol.6, no.3, 1957, pp.7–10 and p.29.

W. Wells, 'Swiss Altar Frontal', *Scottish Art Review*, vol.7, no.1, 1959, pp.18–19 and p.27.

W. Wells, 'Family Pride (Some Heraldic Tapestries in The Burrell Collection)', *Scottish Art Review*, vol.7, no.2, 1959, pp.14-16 and p.28.

W. Wells, 'Picture and Tapestry', *Scottish Art Review*, vol.7, no.3, 1960, pp.26–8.

W. Wells, 'Vice and Folly in Three Swiss Tapestries, *Scottish Art Review*, vol.8, no.2, 1961, pp.13–16.

W. Wells and A. V. B. Norman, 'An Unknown Hercules Tapestry in The Burrell Collection', *Scottish Art Review*, vol.8, no.3, 1962, pp.13–20 and p.32.

W. Wells, 'The Luttrell Table Carpet', *Scottish Art Review*, vol.11, no.3, 1968, pp.14–18, and p.29.

W. Wells, 'The Earliest Flemish Tapestries in The Burrell Collection', *De Bloetijd van de Vlaamse Tapijtkunst*, Brussels, 1969, pp.431–57.

W. Wells, 'Two Burrell Hunting Tapestries', *Scottish Art Review*, vol. XIV, no.1, 1973, pp.10–16.

W. Wells, 'The Marshal Remembers . . . an allegorical view of French History', *Scottish Art Review*, vol. XIV, no.2, 1973, pp.14–21 and p.38.

STAINED GLASS

M. Drake, *The Costessey Collection of Stained Glass*, Exeter, 1920.

J. Dinkel, 'Painting with Light', *Scottish Art Review*, vol. XIV, no.1, 1937, pp.17–19 and p.33.

J. Dinkel, 'Stained Glass from Boppard: New Findings', *Scottish Art Review*, vol. XII, no.2, 1971, pp.22–7.

F. Sydney Eden, 'Ancient Glass at Old Hall, Highgate', *The Connoisseur*, July 1934, 3–8, and August 1934, pp.79–84.

Glasgow Art Gallery and Museum, *Stained and Painted Heraldic Glass in The Burrell Collection*, 1962.

Glasgow Art Gallery and Museum, *Stained and Painted Glass in The Burrell Collection*, 1965.

J. Hayward, 'Stained Glass Windows from the Carmelite Church at Boppard-am-Rhein, a Reconstruction of the Glazing Program of the North Nave', *Metropolitan Museum Journal*, vol.2, 1969, pp.75–114.

W. J. Macaulay, 'French 13th Century Painted Glass in the The Burrell Collection', *Scottish Art Review*, vol. 2, no.4, 1949, pp.13–15.

P. Newton, 'Three Panels of Heraldic Glass in the The Burrell Collection', *Scottish Arts Review*, vol.8, no.4, 1962, pp.13–16.

J. H. Notman, 'The Restoration of a Stained Glass Roundel', *Scottish Art Review*, vol. XIV, no.2, 1973, p.10–13.

S. H. S. Steinberg, 'A Portrait of Beatrix of Falkenburg', *The Antiquaries Journal*, vol.18, no.2, April 1938, pp.140–5.

L. H. Tanner, 'A Rebus of Abbot Islip in The Burrell Collection', *Scottish Art Review*, vol.8, no.4, 1962, pp.9–12 and p.29.

E. von Witzleben, 'Kölner Bibelfenster des 15 Jahrhunderts in Schottland, England und Amerika', *Aachener Kunstblätter*, Bd. 43, 1972, pp.227–48.

W. Wells, 'Stained Glass in The Burrell Collection', *Journal of the British Society of Master Glass Painters*, vol.12, no.4, 1958–9, pp.277–80.

W. Wells, 'Light into Art', *Scottish Art Review*, vol.6, no.2, 1957, pp.32–3.

W. Wells, 'More Light into Art', *Scottish Art Review*, vol.6, no.4, 1958, pp.7–10, and p.29.

W. Wells, 'Stained Glass from Boppard-on-Rhine in The Burrell Collection', *Scottish Art Review*, vol.10, no.3, 1966, pp.22–5.

H. Wentzel, 'Unbekannte Mittelalterliche Glasmalereien der Burrell Collection zu Glasgow', *Pantheon*, May–June 1961, pp.105–113; July–August 1961, pp.173–86; September–October 1961, pp.240–9.

H. Wentzel, 'Eine Glasmalerei-Scheibe aus Boppard in Glasgow', *Pantheon*, 28, 3, 1969, pp.177–81.

METALWORK

I. Finlay, 'Silver in the Collection of Sir William Burrell', *The Connoisseur*, May 1938, pp.242–5.

I. Finlay, 'The Burrell Collection Silver', *Scottish Art Review*, vol.1, no.2, 1946, pp.6–9.

T. D. Kendrick, 'The Temple Pyx', *Antiquaries Journal*, XVI, 1936, pp.51–4.

C. Oman, 'Simon Gribelin', *Apollo*, June 1957, pp.218–21.

WOODWORK

M. Adams-Acton, 'Early English Oak Tables', *The Connoisseur*, December 1936, pp.315–21.

M. Adams-Acton, 'Wall Seats and Settles of the 16th century', *The Connoisseur*, March 1948, pp.16–21.

M. Adams-Acton, 'Early Oak – Recent Additions and Notable Collections', *The Connoisseur*, June 1945, pp.79–85.

M. Adams-Acton, 'The Genesis and Development of Linenfold Panelling', *The Connoisseur*, March 1946, pp.25–31.

A. Hannah, 'Some Early Scottish Chairs', *Scottish Art Review*, vol.5, no.3, 1955, pp.7–10.

E. H. Pinto, 'Early Uses of Lignum Vitae', *Country Life*, 16 September 1965, pp.704–7.

E. H. Pinto, 'Treen Cups for an Exclusive Society', *Country Life*, 30 March 1967, pp.700–1.

W. Wells, 'The Richard de Bury Chest', *Scottish Art Review*, vol.10, no.4, 1966, pp.14–18 and p.31.

NEEDLEWORK

A. Carfax, 'The Elizabethan Relics of Kimberley', *Apollo*, vol.16, 1932–3, p.158.

A. Hannah, 'An Elizabethan Throne', *Scottish Art Review*, vol.2, no.1, 1948, pp.17–18.

W. Wells, 'Heraldic Relics from Kimberley', *Scottish Art Review*, vol.8, no.4, 1962, pp.17–21 and p.31.

SCULPTURE AND IVORY

M. Adams-Acton, 'Medieval Sculpture', *The Connoisseur*, September 1945, pp.3–7.

D. Hall 'A Note on Rodin and the Bronzes in The Burrell Collection', *Scottish Art Review*, vol.11, no.1, 1967, pp.1–5, and p.29.

A. Hannah, 'Virgin and Child', *Scottish Art Review*, vol.5, no.4, 1956, pp.3–5.

W. Wells, 'A Gothic Diptych Reunited', *Scottish Art Review*, vol.11, no.1, 1967, pp.26–8.

PICTURES

Arts Council, *French Paintings of the 19th century from The Burrell Collection*, 1950 (catalogue introduced by Denys Sutton).

M. Bodelson, 'The Missing Link in Gauguin's Cloisonism', *Gazette des Beaux Arts*, May–June, 1959, pp.329–44.

A. Bury, *Joseph Crawhall, the Man and the Artist*, 1958.

Glasgow Art Gallery, *Crawhall in The Burrell Collection*, 1953.

A. Hannah, 'Joseph Crawhall', *Scottish Art Review*, vol.4, no.4, 1953, pp.28–9.

R. L. Herbert, 'Les Faux Millets', *Revue de l'Art*, 21, 1973, pp.56–65.

T. J. Honeyman, 'Degas in The Burrell Collection', *Scottish Art Review*, vol.2, no.4, 1949, pp.8–12.

T. C. Mackie, 'The Collection of Mr. Burrell', *The Studio*, vol.85, no.359, 1923, pp.63–72; vol.85, no.362, 1923, pp.255–61.

T. C. Mackie, 'The Crawhalls of Mr. William Burrell's Collection', *The Studio*, vol.83, no.349, 1922, pp.177–85.

I. Mackintosh, 'Eugène Louis Boudin', *Scottish Art Review*, vol.7, no.3, 1960, pp.24–5.

H. Nef, 'Eine neuentdeckte Ingres-Zeichnung', *Neue Zürcher Zeitung*, Blatt.1, 12 October 1954.

B. Nicolson, 'Courbet's Beggar at Ornans', *Burlington Magazine*, February 1962, pp.1–2.

R. Pickvance, 'Daumier in Scotland', *Scottish Art Review*, vol.12, no.1, 1969, pp.13–16 and p.29.

K. Roberts 'The Date of Degas' "The Rehearsal" in Glasgow', *Burlington Magazine*, June 1963, pp.280–1.

Scottish Arts Council, *A Man of Influence, Alexander Reid, 1854–1928*, 1967 (catalogue of an exhibition compiled and introduced by Ronald Pickvance).

W. R. Sickert, 'Mr. Burrell's Collection at the Tate', *The Southport Visitor*, 1924 (quoted in *Sickert: The Man and his Art; Random Reminiscences*, ed. W. H. Stephenson, 1940).

C. Small, 'Degas' Lenses', *Scottish Art Review*, vol.8, no.4, 1962, pp.1–4.

A. Sturrock, 'The Anecdote Passes', *Scottish Art Review*, vol.7, no.2, 1959, pp.2–5.

D. Talbot Rice, 'Daumier in The Burrell Collection', *Scottish Art Review*, vol.1, no.3, 1947, pp.2–5.

J. P. Weisberg, 'The Works of François Bonvin in The Burrell Collection', *Scottish Art Review*, vol.XIII, no.3, 1972, pp.10–12 and p.31.

W. Wells, 'Degas' Staircase', *Scottish Art Review*, vol.9, no.3, 1964, pp.14–17 and p.29.

W. Wells, 'Géricault in The Burrell Collection', *Scottish Art Review*, vol.9, no.4, 1964, pp.13–17 and p.31.

W. Wells, 'Degas' Portrait of Duranty', *Scottish Art Review*, vol.10, no.1, 1965, pp.18–20 and p.29.

W. Wells, 'The Burrell Collection of French Paintings at Glasgow', *Journal of the Franco-British Society*, vol.XXIX, no.106, 1973, pp.1–3.

W. Wells, 'Variations on a Winter Landscape by Millet', *Scottish Art Review*, vol.XIII, no.4, 1972, pp.5–8 and p.33.

W. Wells, 'Who was Degas' Lyda?', *Apollo*, February 1972, pp.129–34.

J. Wiercinska, 'Theodore Géricault et le "Lancier Polonais" du Musée National de Varsovie' *Bulletin du Musée National de Varsovie*, vol.VIII, no.3, 1967, pp.81–91.

Master of the Brunswick Diptych,
The Annunciation, c. 1485–1490.
(cat. 3)

DVM PVER ALVEOLO FVRATVR MELLA CVPIDO
FVRANTI DIGITVM CVSPITE FIXIT APIS
SIC ETIAM NOBIS BREVIS ET PERITVRA VOLVPTAS
QVAM PETIMVS TRISTI MIXTA DOLORE NOCET.

Lucas Cranach the Elder,
Cupid the Honey Thief complaining to Venus,
1545. (cat. 9)

Giovanni Bellini,
Virgin and Child, c.1488–1490. (cat. 2)

School of Lorraine,
Ecce Homo, c.1470. (cat. 4)

Hans Memlinc,
The Virgin of the Annunciation. (cat. 5)

A. T. Ribot,
The Cooks, 1862. (cat. 42)

F. S. Bonvin, *The Crow*, 1849. (cat. 35)

H. Daumier,
The Miller, his Son and the Ass. (cat. 22)

J. L. A. T. Géricault,
The Polish Trumpeter. (cat. 18)

J. F. Millet,
The Wool Carder, c.1848. (cat. 32)

H. Daumier, *The Bathers*, 1846–48. (cat. 26)

J. D. G. Courbet, *The Washer Women.* (cat. 39)

P. Cézanne, *Le Château de Médan*, c.1880. (cat. 60)

J. D. G. Courbet,
Portrait of Mlle. Aubé de la Holde, 1865.
(cat. 38)

H. G. E. Degas,
Lady with Parasol. (cat. 56)

H. G. E. Degas, *The Rehearsal*, c.1874. (cat. 54)

E. Manet, *Café, Place du Théatre Français.* (cat. 49)

E. Manet,
Marie Colombier, 1880. (cat. 51)

H. G. E. Degas,
Girl looking through Field Glasses. (cat. 53)

H. G. E. Degas, *Portrait of Émile Duranty*, 1879. (cat. 55)

E. Manet, *At the Café*, c.1878. (cat. 48)

A. Sisley, *The Bell Tower, Noisy-le-Roi: Autumn*, 1874. (cat. 59)

J. B. Jongkind, *Fabrique de Cuirs Forts*, 1868. (cat. 41)

H. Fantin-Latour,
Spring Flowers, 1878. (cat. 58)

P. Gauguin,
Breton Girl, c.1886. (cat. 61)

Franco-Burgundian tapestry, *Peasants hunting Rabbits with Ferrets*, c.1460–70. (cat. 81)

Franco-Burgundian tapestry,
*Peasants hunting Rabbits with
Ferrets*, (detail) c.1460–70.
(cat. 81)

Franco-Flemish tapestry, *Mille Fleurs with Charity overcoming Envy*, late 15th or early 16th century. (cat. 91)

German tapestry, *The Pursuit of Fidelity*, c.1475–1500. (cat. 70)

Swiss tapestry panel, *The Wandering House Wife*, third quarter of 15th century. (cat. 74)

Franco-Flemish tapestry, *The Flight of the Heron*, 16th century. (cat. 89)

Franco-Flemish tapestry, *An open-air Meal in the Garden of Love*, c.1510. (cat. 87)

Franco-Flemish tapestry,
An open-air Meal in the Garden of Love,
(detail) c.1510. (cat. 87)

Franco-Flemish tapestry,
*Verdure with arms of
Miro,* (detail) end of 15th
or beginning of 16th
century. (cat. 90)

Franco-Flemish tapestry, *Parc au Cerfs*, c. 1500. (cat. 93)

Franco-Flemish tapestry, *Verdure with arms of Miro*, end of 15th or beginning of 16th century. (cat. 90)

Franco-Flemish tapestry, *The Camel Caravan*, 16th century. (cat. 95)

Franco-Flemish tapestry,
The Camp of the Gipsies,
15th century. (cat. 94)

Franco-Flemish tapestry, *Landscape with Lioness and Doe*, (detail) early 16th century. (cat. 92)

Franco-Flemish tapestry, *Verdure with Thistles*, 15th century. (cat. 96)

Franco-Burgundian tapestry, *Hercules initiating the Olympic Games*, c.1460–70. (cat. 82)

Franco-Flemish tapestry, *Arms of Beaufort, Turenne and Comminges*, 14th century. (cat. 80)

Flemish tapestry fragment,
Beatrix Soetkens in Bed, 1518. (cat. 98)

South German tapestry, *Holy Trinity with the Arma Christi*, c.1420. (cat. 66)

German or Swiss tapestry fragment,
The Visitation, c.1505. (cat. 75)

German tapestry with Wildmen, *Haymaking*, c.1400–25. (cat. 68)

German tapestry fragment, *Three Prophets*, first quarter of 15th century. (cat. 65)

Chinese bronze vessel,
3rd/2nd century B.C.
(cat. 330)

Chinese bronze food vessel, Chou Dynasty, 6th to 5th century B.C. (cat. 327)

Chinese bronze wine bucket,
Western Chou Dynasty, 11th
century B.C. (cat. 324)

Chinese bronze tripod wine vessel,
Chou Dynasty, early 10th
century B.C. (cat. 328)

Chinese Neolithic burial urn. (cat. 298)

Chinese Neolithic burial urn. (cat. 301)

Chinese ewer, Ming, late 14th century. (cat. 320)

Chinese dish, 14th century. (cat. 316)

The Temple Pyx,
German, c.1150. (cat. 371)

Enamelled copper gilt chasse with the
murder of Thomas à Becket,
French, c.1200–1205. (cat. 372)

Enamelled copper gilt pyx, French, 2nd quarter of the 13th century. (cat. 374)

Bronze aquamanile in the form of a lion statant, German, first half 14th century. (cat. 375)

Carved wood group depicting the Lamentation, South German, c.1500. (cat. 368)

Stone roundel carved in high relief, French, c.1260. (cat. 358)

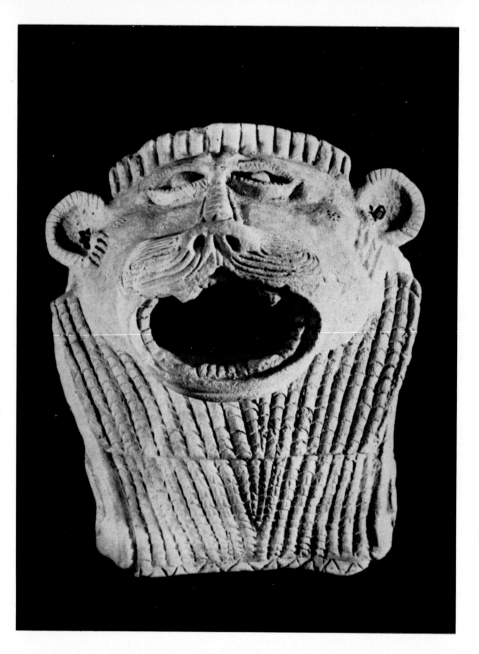

Babylonian(?) terra-cotta lion head,
c.2000–1800 B.C. (cat. 333)

Attic black-figured pottery amphora,
570–550 B.C. (cat. 351)

Egyptian (Old Kingdom) coloured relief fragment, Sixth Dynasty, 2423–2263 B.C. (cat. 343)

Notes on the building for the Burrell Collection, Pollok Park, Glasgow

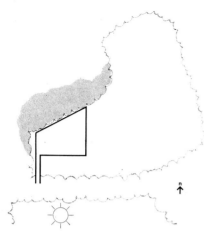

Fig.1

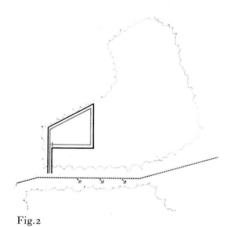

Fig.2

The site is a beautiful green field, rising to the north and set in a dense wood. A small park pavilion at the top of the slope has views to the south and to the hills beyond.

The building is placed in the lower corner of the field alongside the best stand of trees (Fig.1). These trees shield the north wall of the building from direct light enabling that wall to be well glazed and the woodland scene under the trees to be experienced from within the museum. In order to sustain this relationship the Collection is on one level. This creates a building mass that is in sympathy with the scale of the park.

Visitors will arrive from several directions within the park (Fig.2). They may come from Pollok House, which contains the Stirling Maxwell Collection, from across the field in which the building sits – known as the picnic field, or from the park generally. Visitors by car or coach will find parking space along the southern boundary of the site underneath the trees. Inside the building the main route is a simple perimeter walk, where it is possible to view a representative selection of the objects. This route provides a line of reference, and a way of experiencing the Collection as an entity. More detailed studies can be made by lateral movement towards the centre of the building. This kind of organisation may be compared with that of the Victorian museum, where the galleries relate to a large central hall, or with that of the Italian palazzo, where a series of rooms surround one or more courtyards.

The restaurant is placed in the south east corner of the building (Fig.3). It becomes a resting place halfway around the main route, and has sun with views across the field to the surrounding trees.

From the entrance a view of the Hornby portal – an eighteen-foot-high English Renaissance arch – leads the visitor to a glazed courtyard and to the beginning of the Collection (Fig.4). The sunlit court is a gathering place containing trees, seats, and stone sculptures. It also provides daylight and a semi-outdoor world for the three Hutton rooms that surround it. These rooms, the drawing room, hall and dining room are reconstructions of rooms in Hutton Castle, the home of Sir William Burrell, and are furnished in their original manner.

After passing through the arch, the visitor embarks upon 'a walk in the woods' (Fig.5). The first view takes in the ride to the west seen through the two Gothic tracery windows. From then on the main route leads the visitor through a series of large open spaces containing a selection of art objects from antiquity, from Turkey, Persia, India and China, and from Europe. Further investigation of the Collection would lead the visitor away from the main route, through a sequence of different spaces, to the long tapestry gallery at the heart of the building. It is anticipated that the collection of tapestries and the woodland scene will be complementary, and that an exploration of the Collection will link

Fig.3

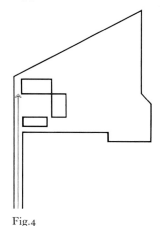

Fig.4

them. The main route then returns down the east side of the building, through the picture gallery into the corner overlooking the restaurant and views to the park. Leading off the gallery are rooms for 16th, 17th and 18th century arrangements of the Collection. Silverware, glassware, ceramics and metalwork are displayed along the south side of the building. The south wall is glazed, and against this bright light is shown the extensive collection of religious and armorial stained glass.

A lecture theatre for 250 people and a space for frequently changing exhibitions separate the north and south display areas. It is possible to close off the northern major display space, so that the lecture theatre, exhibition space and restaurant can become a place for meetings after regular museum hours (Fig.6).

A first floor mezzanine for specialised study overlooks the north area and the tapestry gallery. Walkways link this mezzanine to offices at the same level along the south side of the building. Stairs and lifts in the centre of the building connect this level with the restorers' floor on the roof, the ground floor and the basement. The basement contains storage space for the objects not currently on display, and the air-conditioning plant, and at a lower ground floor level the workshops, kitchen and restaurant.

The building as far as possible uses natural materials. It is fully air-conditioned to control the temperature, humidity and purity of the air. All natural light passes through ultra-violet filters and its quality – its direction and intensity, is controlled by rolling blinds. Apart from the perimeter spaces and three daylit galleries which penetrate into the interior of the museum, the museum is artificially lit.

In conclusion, we have tried to pursue the following thoughts:
Firstly, we wish to resolve in the building the conflict between, on the one hand, the rare opportunity of enjoying a superb park, and on the other, the demands of conservation which require that many of the objects in the Collection be protected from the natural light of that world. The former consideration tends to make the building open, the latter closed. The park provides a context for display, and as such poses the issue of the relationship between art and nature.

Secondly, we wish to create a variety of opportunities for display. In a collection of this size there will obviously be a basic order for arranging the objects so that they can be comprehended, yet we hope that if there is a variety of places in the building the qualities of place might suggest the location of an object instead of order. Thus we hope that we can generate informality and surprise, and that the building will assume some of the characteristics of house as well as museum, as was Sir William's wish.

Thirdly, there is posed the issue of the nature of objects in a museum.

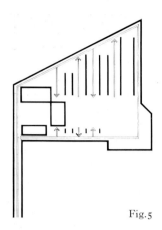

Fig.5

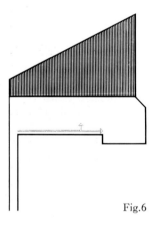

Fig.6

How does one display a stone portal which was once a doorway and is now a piece of sculpture, which was once outdoors and is now indoors? What is a piece of stained glass that once had location and message, and now has history and is preserved forever? How does one display objects of one epoch in a building that denies many of the qualities of that epoch? How does one resolve the relationship of objects that are very explicit to a building that tends not to be, and how does one, oneself, relate to objects when of necessity protection from light, air and touch intervene in that experience.

Barry Gasson
February 1975

Site model view from the east

North walk looking west

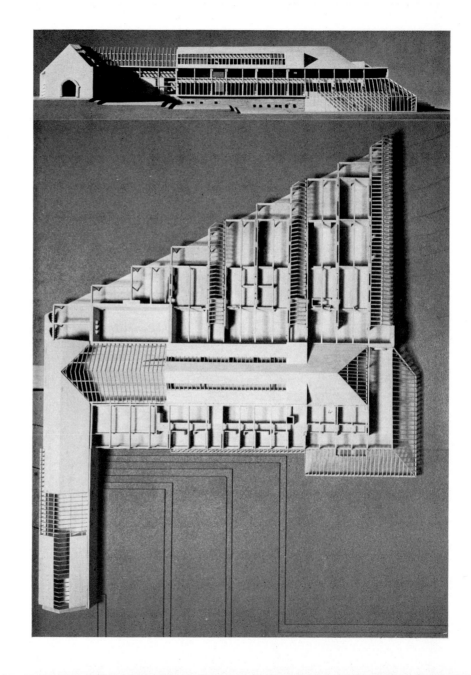

Two views of the model of the building:
south elevation and view from the top